Salon style

Salon-style

FICTION POETRY & ART

edited by
Brian Centrone

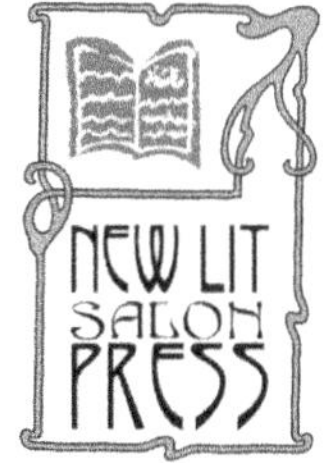

The NEW Series by New Lit Salon Press

Southern Gothic: New Tales of The South edited by Brian Centrone & Jordan M. Scoggins
Behind the Yellow Wallpaper: New Tales of Madness edited by Rose Yndigoyen
Startling Sci-Fi: New Tales of the Beyond edited by Casey Ellis

Other titles by New Lit Salon Press

I Voted for Biddy Schumacher: Mismatched Tales from the Mind of Brian Centrone
Retrospective by Michael Tice
Erotica by Brian Centrone

Salon Style

Published by New Lit Salon Press, 2014

Edited by Brian Centrone
Line Edited by Casey Ellis
Design and handwriting by luke kurtis

Dan Ress's "Room for Rent" first appeared in *Imaginaire Magazine*, November 30, 2013.
Stefanie Freele's "Hankering" first appeared in *Feeding Strays: Short Stories by Stefanie Freele*, Lost Horse Press, 2009.
Jessica Hoard's *Patterson #2* first appeared in *Greatest Uncommon Denominator*, Issue #3, Autumn 2008.
Several of the works by Michael Tice originally appeared in *Retrospective*, New Lit Salon Press, 2013.

New Lit Salon Press
Carmel, NY

ISBN 978-0-9972649-1-3

www.newlitsalonpress.com

Table of Contents

Crawl Space

M.P. Diederich • 9

The Bus Ride

John Rodzvilla • 21

Room for Rent

Dan Ress • 26

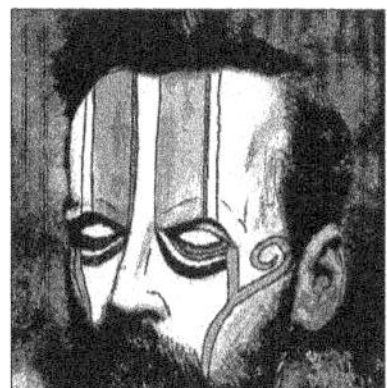

Heavier Things

Carrion House • 33

Breakfast of Champions • Oni Gent • When The Windws Turned 10 • Glass Passenger • The Rescue Blues • Against The Rain • Shapes and Sizes • Rain Mouth • Dragon Clothes • Blossom Bridge • Blood Hands • Clown Force • Waiting For Superman

Ms Suburbia

Michele Seminara • 47

Mary

Reymond Drew • 50

Hankering

Stefanie Freele • 54

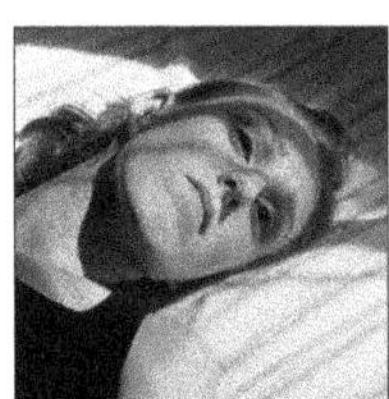

Still, She Rises

Jessica Hoard • 57

Self Portrait 1 • Creeper • The Zig and the Zag • An Exquisite Cage • Around the Corner Down the Corridor • Patterson #2 • Patterson #1 • Self Portrait • Cossitt Library • Manchester • Twisted • Web • The Weight • The Rabbit Hole • In Shadow • Momentum • Into the Fog • The Spiral Staircase • Flowers

The Three Chagalls

John Vicary • 78

The Creature from the Lake

Casey Ellis • 83

The Dust Gets Into Everything

Jack Bates • 90

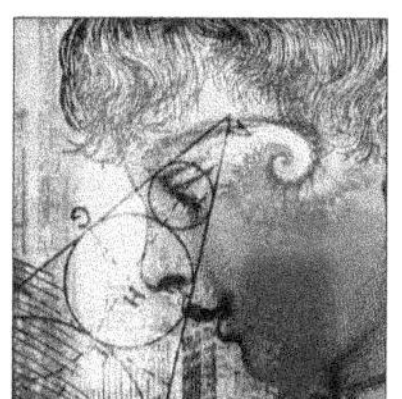

Universal Assemblage

Nathan Mark Phillips • 101

Attack of the Drones • Planetary Contemplations • Aliens Among Us # • Aliens Among Us #2 • Aliens Among Us #1 • Looking for Love on Mars • Observing Earth • All's Fair in Love and War • Wanting to Fly

Fire Thirst

P.J. Scheafer • 111

I'll Take Ashes

P.J. Scheafer • 116

Anarchical Borderline Child

Sarah-Jean Krahn • 122

Not All In Mees Head • Mees A Person

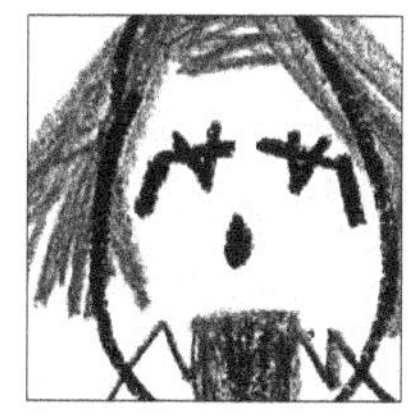

Four Poems

Michael Algera • 126

How I Returned Here • Sandals and Socks • Talent • Pizza Deliverance

Madame Strange

Lucy Black • 135

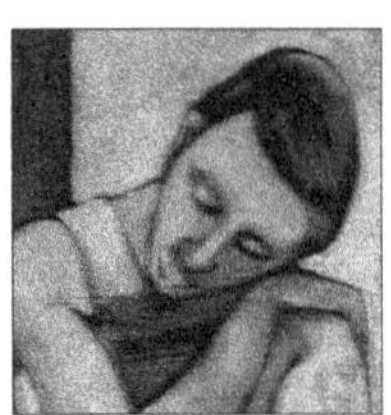

A Selection of Works on Paper & Canvas

Michael Tice • 143

Curiosity • Summer Reverie • N.Y. Blues • Portrait Study • Memory Lain • Fairweather Friend • Untitled • Dream State

Crawl Space

M.P. Diederich

It should come as no surprise that, in the grand scheme of American employment, exterminators have it pretty rough. George Wanzenmorder took this in stride, though; it was not in his nature to complain, and, in his estimation, he was providing a much-needed, valuable service to the world. After all, no one enjoys the sudden shock, followed by the spine-tingling ripple of revulsion that results from the glimpse of a fat, shiny roach scurrying by behind the kitchen sink.

There were also certain characteristics of George's personality that suited him to an exterminator's work. For one, the bugs themselves never really bothered him, not even from the first job. He learned that many of the older veterans in the company had had to overcome their initial hibbly-jibblies as regards large insects of the genus *periplaneta*. George, on the other hand, never had such issues—not even on his very first assignment, when he found himself literally knee-deep in roaches in that veritable shithole down on Rivington Street.

"Most dudes don't recover from that kind of shit," said Larry, the senior operator he'd accompanied, as they rinsed the legs and wings off their boots. "You may work out yet, George."

Larry explained the concept of what he'd taken to calling "Subshock"—a pseudo-Freudian type of paranoid neurosis in which the sufferer (usually a rookie exterminator) begins to manifest an abject terror of pulling back curtains, opening doors, or removing the lid from any sort of container or compartment. When you've waded through literal puddles of cockroaches, removed kitchen stoves to discover entire cities of vermin, pulled up floorboards to find species of water bug you thought only existed in science-fiction films from the 1950s...well, let's just say you're bound to lose control of your imagination when it begins to consider the dark, vile world that exists just below the surface of everything around you. Those poor sons of bitches (the Subshocked) rarely made it past their first week on the job, and were never the same again.

What suited George best to his work was his love of the problem-solving aspects of extermination. With little more than determination and a pressurized tank full of toxic chemicals, one service technician could wipe out an entire colony of German cockroaches in a matter of hours. But it was the big jobs that really got George's blood boiling—the massive infestations. The houses where rats had, for all intents and purposes, replaced the original insulation material. The refrigerators that seemed to be doing the hustle in the corner of the kitchen, just from the movement of the six-legged residents dwelling around the warmth of the condensing coils. The mildewy carpet that rippled independent of any outside influence—and trust me, you do *not* want to look under the couch. George always volunteered for these jobs.

For ten years, George was practically a legend for his feats of anti-arthropod and anti-rodent conquest. His eye for the tiniest traces of insect fecal matter, the slightest hint of tearing in the drywall, the tell-tale signs of shed exoskeleton under the baseboard—it was extolled as a positively Sherlockian talent. Rumor had it that simply uttering his name was enough to send the little vermin scuttling off to hiding places deep in the sewer. Needless to say, when the new owner of a dilapidated old manse in the suddenly revived stretch of Brooklyn blight known as Gowanus needed the best in the business, it didn't take her long to find out that the first, last, and practically only name in the pest control business was George Albert Wanzenmorder.

Miss Ellen Lupus knew full well what she was getting into by buying the old Thornbee place. The last of the old family—one of those minor Gilded Age dynasties that lost everything in the Crash of '29—had left the house to the dogs some time in the late 1950s. Situated on the corner of Third Avenue and Bethel Street—just a few blocks from the pungent, soupy sludge of the Gowanus Canal—the old Thornbee place had been a boarded-up eyesore among boarded-up eyesores for as long as anyone could remember. The area surrounding the old manse was so desolate it couldn't even be considered dangerous, let alone desirable. For the better part of six decades, the Thornbee place became more and more overgrown, its walls stained and mushy. Even for the brief period in the 1970s when a group of junkie squatters took up long-term residence there, the place had more the appearance of a peculiar rock formation covered in vines and moss than any sort of manmade construction. But still, there was something about this Italianate manse nestled in the midst of an abandoned industrial zone that was simply irresistible to Ellen Lupus who, through various inquiries and finagling with the city government, was able to acquire the old Thornbee place for next to nothing.

Of course, years of disrepair, disuse, and exposure to the elements had left the place little more than a shell of the luxurious palace that Aldous Thornbee had constructed in the sleepy outskirts of 19th Century Brooklyn. Ellen Lupus had called a number of contractors to take a look at the sagging roof and the cracks in the foundation, but the preponderance of creepy, crawling things slinking around in the walls and ceilings and floorboards of the moldy, swollen old manse proved too much for even the most seasoned veterans of the construction industry. In her usual thorough and diligent way, Ellen found just the man for the job of evicting the innumerable previous tenants of her new home.

George arrived early in the morning for the initial inspection; his assistant, Carlton, sat slumped over, snoring in the passenger seat of the van.

"Good morning," said the young woman in the houndstooth pant suit, standing at the front gate with a cigarette in her left hand. "You must be Mr. Wanzenmorder."

"And you must be Ellen Lupus," said George. He elbowed Carlton in the ribs; the younger man jumped up and immediately clamored out of the van to start unloading equipment out of the back.

The three of them entered the once-grand hall of the old manse—now reduced to a dank, mold-stained cavern of rotting beams and bulging boards. The whole room stank of decay, and felt more like a mausoleum than a home.

"As you can see," said Ellen Lupus, "there's still a lot of work to be done. Fortunately, the foundation is still pretty solid, and most of the structure is brick and concrete. I'm not all that concerned with the termite damage."

"Have you noticed any visible signs of infestation?" asked George, pointing his flashlight along the edges of the floor, searching for signs of activity.

"Surprisingly, no," said Ellen. "At least, nothing more than the occasional rat or roach in the upper rooms. The real problem is down in the basement."

George nodded. This sort of thing was quite common, he'd found, in reclamation projects such as this one. Naturally accustomed to wet, dark, warm places, the average roach generally sticks to the basement. Considering the building's history of abandonment, there was really no telling what one was liable to find down there.

Ellen led George and Carlton to the rear of the manse, through a massive kitchen and pantry (both stripped bare of anything of possible value), and to a small vestibule at the back, where an ancient wooden door, green with moss and latched closed with rusted iron hinges, clung to the cellar doorway.

"I know your reputation, Mr. Wanzenmorder," said Ellen, "and I'm well aware of your experience with all sorts of infestation. You've probably seen much worse than whatever's on the other side of the door here, but I will still warn you that the building inspector I brought in to look at the foundation screamed like a little girl when he looked down there."

George smiled at her. In his experience, building inspectors had very weak stomachs for the truly terrible manifestations of cockroach colonization.

"Shall we?" said Ellen.

George and Carlton readied their flashlights and aerosol cans of roach spray; Ellen undid the latch, and with a heavy, creaking groan the cellar door swung open. George and Carlton shined their flashlights down the concrete stairway, which descended some thirty feet. To all of their surprise, the stairs appeared clean and intact—not a single roach in sight. George went first, followed closely by Ellen and Carlton.

Scritchscritchscritch.

"Do you hear that?" whispered Carlton.

George did, and held a finger to his lips.

They reached the bottom of the stairs, where they found a veritable sea of roaches, undulating and rippling in an almost hypnotic pattern. The mass of insects stretched across the whole floor of the basement, even reaching up the walls to the ceiling overhead. It was pretty bad, but as far as sheer numbers, George had seen worse.

"This is disgusting," said Carlton. "No disrespect, Miss Lupus."

"There's just…so many of them," said Ellen.

"It's not the number that worries me," said George, kneeling down to spray one of the few roaches by his feet. He watched one writhe and flail out the last painful seconds of its life, then examined the corpse closely in the light of his flashlight. "Yeah, this is a weird one," he said. "See this?" he said, pointing to the long, thin antennae of the dead roach. "This is an American cockroach. Also known as the Palmetto bug. Generally one of the more common species of cockroach. Now, normally when you have infestation on this level, you're dealing with the German cockroach—slightly smaller than this fella here, with a very different coloration on its wings. The German roach is more prone to colonization, which results in the type of massive population you see here. The American roach? Not so much. In fact, the American roach is more of a loner—a solitary scavenger in search of a wet, dark pile of garbage. In my professional opinion, this massive colony of American roaches here in your basement is cause for alarm."

"Great," said Ellen. "What do we do about it?"

"We spray the living fuck out of 'em," said Carlton, priming the small tank of roach spray on his back. "If you'll pardon my French."

"Are you sure you have enough of that stuff to…" Ellen paused in the middle of the sentence and followed George's gaze to the vast sea of roaches which, to everyone's alarm, had suddenly stopped its undulation. Every one of the roaches now stood stock still, antennae stiff and perked up, each of their beady little cockroach eyes pointed directly at Carlton and his tank of poison.

"Well," said Carlton. "I'll be damned."

"Should I be concerned?" asked Ellen.

"I don't know," George admitted. "I've never seen the likes of this, but I doubt anything good can come of it."

"We're gonna need a lot more dust than we got," said Carlton.

A rhythmic chirping sound began to rise from the insect multitude before them—a pulsing, shrill throb, like the cockroaches were chanting. The chirps began softly, then grew in volume and pitch until the whole basement vibrated with the shrieking of the thousands upon thousands of roaches. Ellen took a step backward toward the stairs; George and Carlton assumed defensive postures.

"What the fuck are they doing?" Carlton yelled above the deafening shrieks of the amassed army.

George was about to say "I have no idea," when, with a flutter of wings and a shrill, unified cry, wave upon wave of cockroaches began flying toward them. Ellen ran for the stairs while George and Carlton sprayed wildly in all directions, felling hundreds of roaches as they darted toward them.

The sprays and powders proved not to be enough. Despite their best efforts, the endless waves of fluttering insects kept up the relentless assault. They managed to make it through the cloud of gaseous death and landed all up and down Carlton and George's bodies.

"Fucking hell!" yelled Carlton. "They're fucking biting me!"

George clawed and swiped and smashed at the roaches, then darted toward the stairs. Oddly, the roaches seemed to fall away without a fight once he reached the steps. The few that still clung to him were easily squashed or swatted away. George began to climb the stairs, rapidly ascending to the light two steps at a time. Then, back over his shoulder behind him, he heard Carlton's screams for help.

George ran back down the steps and saw, to his horror, Carlton's flailing body covered head-to-toe with thousands of scurrying, furious roaches. The spray equipment was nowhere to be found, and the spray can in George's hand was useless against such numbers. Paralyzed by his helplessness and transfixed by the sight before him, George watched as the army of roaches continued to swarm over Carlton's body, which staggered drunken-like amid the revolting horde. Carlton's screams and pleas were muffled now by the bodies of roaches, crawling into his mouth and down his throat in an effort to suffocate him. Finally, Carlton's roach-ridden form collapsed to the floor, where George watched the now-lifeless body, overthrown by the hideous mass of slick, brown bugs, disappear into the thick carpet of crawling roaches. Unable to truly believe what he'd just witnessed, George turned and fled back up the long staircase, up to the bright surface world, and slammed the rotten, green door behind him.

The very next day, George sold his truck and all his equipment. After what he had seen, there was no way that George, despite his vast experience and knowledge of the trade, could possibly continue as an exterminator. The calls kept coming for a few months, as homeowners and even fellow exterminators pleaded in vain for George to rejoin the fight. It was no use, he told them; there just wasn't any way to defeat the roaches.

Due to his previous success, as well as the considerable profit he'd turned from the sale of his business, George was able to live quite comfortably over the next ten years, purchasing a small apartment in Carroll Gardens—just a short walk from the old Thornbee place (which, as it turns out, remains dilapidated and abandoned). To pass the time, George took a part-time job as a conductor on the F train. Most of his evenings were spent in his living room, watching the Yankees on television. It wasn't the most exciting way to enter one's autumn years, but George felt lucky nonetheless. After all—it could have been him under that pile of loathsome assailants, torn apart from inside by an army of cockroaches.

It was a rather cool evening in September when George first noticed them. They were just simple streaks of brown material; to the untrained eye, they'd go entirely unnoticed. George, however, knew exactly what they were, and he began to search the darker corners of his kitchen, behind the stove and under the refrigerator. Alas, not a trace.

A few weeks passed. One night found George sitting in the living room, watching a rather unremarkable Yankees-Mariners game in which the Bombers had gone comfortably ahead on a Chip Barksdale grand slam in the sixth. Hungry from boredom, and in need of a second beer, George roused himself from the comfort of the couch and headed to the kitchen.

He flipped on the light switch and there they were: at least thirty fat, brown cockroaches, all lined up in a rigid formation, like a Spartan phalanx defending the pass at Thermopylae. Even in the bright light they stood their ground, motionless except for the odd waving of their long, spindly antennae. A chill ran down George's spine; for ten years he had never been able to get the sound out of his head—that deafening cry of the cockroach horde, nor the pathetic, helpless screams of poor Carlton as the terrible things tore his body apart.

George stood still in the doorway, staring down at the neat little regiment of roaches between him and the refrigerator. He took a step toward them; they moved an inch forward. George took a step to his right; the roaches countered by shuffling an inch in the same direction. He screamed at them; they hissed loudly en masse and waved their antennae. Finally, George leapt forward, not wanting to let them gain the element of surprise. *Homo sapiens vs. periplaneta Americana, mano a mano.*

He stomped the first few rows; the back ranks of the cockroach phalanx shrieked and flew toward him, up onto his legs and began scurrying upward. George spat and cursed and flung the roaches off his body, stomping and kicking and flailing and mashing furiously, smearing their horrible, gooey insides all across the linoleum floor. Finally, George emerged victorious—29 kills in all, crushed and mushy and pulverized all over the floor. The last of the insect regiment lay on its back before him—its thorax burst open, oozing its rotten, trash-fed, roachy guts onto the floor. Still, the cockroach flung its forelegs into the air, angrily punching with its tiny cockroach fists, defiant to the last. George slowly lowered his foot onto the cockroach's writhing body, and a smile stretched over his face as he crunchily dispatched the wounded survivor of the battle.

For weeks, George kept a lookout for more of the militarized roaches, obsessively scouring every inch of the apartment in an effort to deprive the fiendish little freeloaders of any trace of sustenance. He stocked up on cans of Raid, waiting for a second assault that seemed to never come. Maybe that was the end of it, George thought. After all, he'd beaten them outright, leaving no survivors to tell the tale.

Returning home from his shift on the F train one night, George had barely given a thought to the battle with the tiny roach phalanx for some weeks. Tired from a long day on his feet, George tossed his jacket on the couch and went to the kitchen to grab a beer from the fridge. When he flipped on the light, his stomach lurched in terror.

There were hundreds of them—all lined up in perfect ranks, twenty across and at least two dozen deep. They hissed up at him, waving their antennae threateningly. George glimpsed the can of Raid in the pantry just to his left, and quickly grabbed it. The formation of roaches took a step forward, hissing loudly.

George let out a bloodcurdling battle cry and fired the Raid into their ranks, spraying dozens and dozens of roaches in a fog of death. He watched with a beaming grin as they stopped in their tracks, flipped onto their backs, and clawed in vain at the poisonous mixture burning out their eyes, mouths, and other orifices. The survivors charged forward, but George kept up the steady stream of poisonous spray and massacred wave after wave of attacking roaches.

Before long, the cockroaches began to back down, rapidly retreating toward the darker corners of the kitchen. George hollered at them, swore and damned them and their vile race to the deepest pit of Hell. All round his feet lay the scattered corpses of his vanquished foes—legs curled upward, lifeless and still. George smiled. Victory seemed complete as he watched the last of the roaches scurry under the stove. He was about to turn back toward the pantry to fetch the broom and dustpan when he heard a sound that shook him to the very core.

SCRITTTCCHSSSCRRITTTCCHHHSCRRITTTCCHHH…

It was coming from all around him—inside the walls and in the ceiling and from under the linoleum floor

SCRRRRITTTCHSSCRRRRITTCCHSSSSCRRRITTTTCHHH…

"Oh god…" George said aloud.

From all corners of the room they began to march in with straight, disciplined columns, two abreast. There had to be thousands of them—at least as many as he'd seen that fateful day inside the basement of the old Thornbee manse. The roach columns assembled themselves into tiny brigades in the center of the room, all facing toward George, awaiting the ex-exterminator's next move.

George shook the can of Raid; it was nearly empty now. How could the roaches be doing this, he wondered? An intense wave of nausea overcame him. He thought again of poor Carlton, screaming as the roaches overtook him. The vast army of cockroaches now arrayed in George's kitchen were even more organized, more alert than those that had devoured his poor assistant on that horrible morning. They stood their ground, antennae upright and alert. They were ready for a full-on battle.

He knew he couldn't win—not this time. He needed more firepower.

"All right," George said to the cockroaches; "you win."

He backed away, out of the kitchen. The roach brigades marched forward to the threshold of the kitchen doorway, stopping just a few inches from the tips of George's shoes. George flipped off the light switch and turned back toward the hall toward his bedroom. Though it was probably just his imagination, he could have sworn he heard a rousing cheer go up from the victorious periplanetic army in the kitchen.

The Bus Ride

John Rodzvilla

It starts on a cross-town bus in the winter. I hate taking buses in the winter; they never stick to a schedule and the heaters are usually broken or so weak that only the first few seats behind the driver escape the permafrost creeping up the aisles. But it never has more than seven or eight passengers and it beats taking the subway back into the city only to grab the over-stuffed local by the library.

During the summer there's never a problem; the sun stays out until seven so I can read while waiting and the benches aren't hidden in snow banks. But winter's darkness arrives before I can make it out of the office and the weather turns the bus schedule into a crapshoot. What usually happens is that I'm walking to the closest stop on Kendall when the bus passes me and I see the giant aquamarine "C" on the side and know it only stops to discharge and pick-up, unlike the locals that sit there for ten minutes. I run the block and a half, feel the cold air cut into my lungs and, if I'm lucky, hit the tail end of the queue and a ride home. Otherwise, I'll stand for 30 minutes and squint to read by the neon light emanating from the food court.

Today I achieved the often-dreamed psychic bus-sense. At around 6:45 I started getting jittery, stopped debugging the code that had wasted my day and grabbed my coat. As I walked out of the underground parking lot near the stop, the turquoise C turns the corner. I'm there as the doors open. The bus has about 13 people in it (big night) most of them take up the double seats on the right or the benches that run for 3 seats behind the bus driver. I grab one of the few singles left and pull out my book. It's a short story collection called Along the Charles. The stories are about unrequited love and forbidden nights in the large houses that are now used by Boston University to house administration offices and god knows what else. Several stories end with the characters moving to Manhattan or drowning in the Charles. Seems the author's read too much Goethe and wants to bring young Werther into the 21st century. It's not great writing, but it's compelling enough (probably add that to my GoodReads review).

I start a story called "Hell's Half Acre." It's about a group of Harvard students that go ice fishing during the winter intercession and one wanders off only to fall under the ice. You never really hear about people drowning in the Charles now. It's not as if the river's completely inaccessible. Rusted iron ladders lead down to the water every half-mile on the Cambridge side and there's nothing to stop you from just walking in from the Esplanade. Of course if you're even going to attempt it you've got to get past the brackish muck and nasty slick skin of the water. It looks like elephant skin when the sunlight hits it in the summer and it's frozen all winter. Still, I never see any signs of parties on the ice.

I'm sitting in one of those molded blue plastic seats bolted into the side of the bus. I'm a little too short so my feet sway over the floor with the stopping and starting of rush hour traffic. In ten minutes my lower back is throbbing from the unnatural fit. After a few pages I look up and realize that we haven't moved that much. Traffic is clogging the rotary. Ahead is a massive curve of cars, idling and inching forward across lanes in an attempt to exit to the bridge or edge toward the on-ramp to Soldier's Field Road. By the time the bus hits the rotary I've started another story. This one is about a college student who meets a stranger at night walking through one of the alleys in the Back Bay. The stranger turns out to be the ghost of an early seafarer who lived in 18th century Boston and was chased out of the city into the marshland where he was beaten unconscious and left to drown when the tide came in. Just as I get into the reason for the haunting the lights flicker and go out. I try to read by holding the book straight up in front of me to catch the mustard glow of the streetlights along the side of the road.

It's no use. I close the book and just stare out at the red tail-lights that make a necklace around the rotary. Reminds me of a puzzle I had when I was young where you needed to move pieces around to get wooden arcs to make a circle. I hated that game. Never solved it.

My right leg is asleep and I start flexing it against the chair brace to get the blood flowing.

Ten minutes in the rotary in the dark. I can't believe this. I can walk across the bridge faster than this traffic, but the bus driver won't let us out. Some guy went up about 5 minutes ago and tried to get out. Bus driver called him crazy, saying he wasn't going to let anyone out into the middle of traffic. The guy pointed out that the traffic's not moving. The driver pointed out that he couldn't open the doors with the cars jammed so tightly. They were at an impasse. The guy sat down in a seat at the front of the bus and even in near total darkness I can see him glare back at the driver. He has nothing to do but wait.

What was that? Behind me I hear a quick gurgle and what sounds like the zip of corduroy. For some reason it makes me uneasy. I debate looking behind me for several minutes. Every so often I hear someone shift in their seat and a ragged inhale of breath. The bus is starting to give me a case of the willies. I sit up straight. Listening. For what? I can't look back. I don't want to look back. I feel a slight breeze on my arm hair. Muscles tense and I turn to look back. There's no one there.

Wait. There were at least thirteen people behind me when we left Kendall. Now I can only see seven.

I close my eyes and a cinematic outpouring of fear—vampires, zombies and murderers—plays across my lids. Giant nebulous creatures move over the chairs, faintly glowing in the darkness, suffocating the other riders before consuming them. I turn again and see something out of the corner of my eye. A gelatinous mass? Smog? Ether? A partially-digested skull floating in a luminescent cloud? Tendons melt away; the jaw wobbles and then falls as if it were laughing at me before I too come apart while waiting to get over the bridge.

I sit there waiting for the final moment—the denouement of this movie. I sit and wait as we edge onto the bridge. Down below the river rocks back and forth in its elephant skin picking up the lights from BU and something slips through the ice, moving down and out towards the bay.

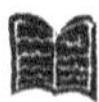

Room for Rent

Dan Ress

The room's story is as strange as its construction. The story is full of bizarre permutations of character and circumstance, swirling like so many shadows, absences set into the backdrop and deepening one another. The construction involves such unlikely dimensions as to bespeak a forbidden branch of calculus derived only to construct this room, and then forgotten. In one corner, two angles meet to forge a perfect polyhedron, curved and meaningful, bowing to no old gods or laws of geometry and form. Spiraling out are arms of inequalities exclusive of one another, gaps and holes filling space with beam and board. And what wood could grow such textures, such raw colors, never painted, or if painted never kept painted, the surfaces too slick for paint to stick, what wood could carve or be carved or grow or be grown to participate in such madness? No mortar could keep the joints, no nails could hold the impossible holdings of space and time forced unnaturally into this sequence. The room is bigger on the inside than on the outside, yet cloying and binding, like a limit set to define not just its own boundaries but those of any that set foot inside.

The mad architect who designed the place must have killed herself after its construction, one assumed upon entering, if ever an architect existed mad enough to dream such a design, let alone to realize it. Perhaps the architect is still dreaming, through the sleep of death, or even stillborn but dreaming a world unbounded by experience; a dream might explain the Eschered rails and staircases implied by the room's unprecedented surfaces and sudden slopes. Perhaps indeed there was no architect, but rather the place exists only out of necessity, because of the utmost extreme end of the infinite curve of probability, an extreme that must exist somewhere, for absurdity must exist in order for rationality to have any meaning, and indeed that curve seems to have rainbowed down just to this room with no pot of gold but for the gilded sense of wonder that forces eyes to inspect the plain floors or walls or ceilings until they run out of light, left sputtering in the darkness of what they beheld. Somehow it is more comforting to think of this construction as unconstructed, unbuilt, as simply existing and apt to stop existing or to reorder in the span of a head turn, spinning insideways to leave a more wholesome chamber surrounding the turner's head. And somehow, I think that is how the room's story, unfinished, incomplete, is bound to end, but not before it flexes its power a bit more, rips just deeper into the collective subconscious through its meager access points, those few of such luck to enter, most of whom even leave to spread tales of the room, none of them true, but all strangely affecting. This is my tale.

When I found the room, I needed quarters for a month during which I would conduct my research on some writer, a poet or philosopher, it does not matter which, by delving into the small wealth of material, unsorted and esoteric, maintained by his estate. The writer was concerned with the nature of Truth, and while I thought I knew what that meant, I was also pretty sure that no one really did.

After some searching, I noticed the faded "For Rent" sign on the post just across and down the street, having had no luck so far in finding the cheap, short-term lodgings I'd sought. I called the number, spoke to a gravelly, disembodied voice across an unknown gap in space and time, and agreed to terms and a showing later that day.

I stopped for lunch at a local sandwich place, turkey with bacon on a Kaiser roll (isn't it strange which details you remember years after, miles away, some you should have forgotten, some that you know ought to still remain but have drifted off, leaving only dust and shadowed gaps?), and met the voice outside the building around two o'clock. No longer disembodied, the voice was still far from reassuring.

"I haven't had much luck with renters," it said.

"Well, I haven't had much luck with landlords," I countered awkwardly. The voice's eyes informed me I'd made a mistake. "Just joking," I added, choked and to little avail.

"That's why I'm willing to consider a monthly rate, instead of keeping it to annual cases." I really didn't care for the use of the word "cases," or the slight emphasis on the word. That really sticks out in my memory.

"Well I'm happy enough to keep my case to a month, no problems here." It really was an awkward conversation. "I mean, the price is right, right?"

"Yeah, about that. I do need it all up front. So, do you have it?"

"Of course." Something in the voice's eyes made me hedge. "Uh, I mean, not on me, but of course I'll give it to you later today. If I like the room. Can we check it out?"

The voice grimaced, sighed, as though its trap had almost snapped shut around me, but I had somehow jammed a bone or a branch between its jaws and hopped out at the last moment. Now it might go hungry.

"As you say. This way." The voice led me up a few flights of stairs, which creaked in an unusual way, sort of like an out of tune guitar, except, well, stairs creaking.

There was only one room on this floor, not the top, but somehow the smallest, like some giant had pinched the building, squeezed it between his thumb and forefinger. The voice opened the door, and I walked inside, and I stared. I'm not sure how long I stared. I'm not totally sure that I'm not still staring, seeing everything that has followed in some crevice between two boards that should never have been able to connect in that way. When I came to, or at least when I think I came to, the voice was talking.

"…and make sure to lock up when you leave. We've had an increase in burglaries the last few years." I can't imagine a person breaking into that room, even through a widely open front door, and stealing anything, ever.

"Uh, y-yes, of course," I managed, mouth still agape.

"And you won't be having any gentleman callers…?"

"Uh, no, of course, no, I mean—"

"Good. Because I run a Christian house." Who in God's name would bring anyone over to this place, Christian or any other religion? And for that matter, no god had power here, it was obvious. How could a god rule over a place that broke all of her rules so blatantly?

"Yes, of course. Well, uh, everything seems in order,"—in the loosest sense of the term—"So I'm anxious to get moved in, get started on my research."

"That's right, you mentioned you're a student." The voice implied that such was an ignoble pursuit.

"No, not so much. I mean, well, yes, but only at university. I mean, it's doctoral research."

The voice's eyes spoke volumes, indicting the entire bastion of academia both for allowing the existence of such nonsense generally and also specifically for affording such a babbling idiot a place in its high ranks. "Yes. Well, just make sure I have the rent by six tonight. We'll sign the papers then, too. If there's nothing else, I'll see you once you have your things, and my money." The voice didn't beat around the bush.

We parted ways, and later that night I signed and paid and took the keys. Then I moved in. Did I ever really move out?

The next month passed strangely, with amazing speed and focus. I had never worked so hard, or focused so much. My subject seemed to be moving closer and closer under my lens, deeper and deeper into my understanding. I was so close now, so deep. The Truth was almost tangible just outside my grasp. I needed more time, so I signed up for another month. The really strange thing though, what I should have noticed, was that I never actually made it over to the poet or philosopher's estate to look at the material. Rather, I stayed in the room and researched; instead of venturing out, I turned inward, and investigated what the great thinker meant through the insane whorls in the room's southwest corner, which seemed to point towards the rising sun, as did my subject's ideas; they pointed and curled together with the room, and so did I. And on the other side, the East let the calculations continue on their own, like pi or god or time, and all the time, facing the South, the writer sat smiling, and I was so close to understanding why, I just needed more time, so I signed up for yet another month.

I decided a more systematic approach was necessary during that third month, so by the end of it, I signed up for another six, despite a really touching note of concern from the voice ("Are you sure?"—Yeah. "Okay, then. If you're sure. All in advance still."). I investigated each grain in the unearthly wood, wound with it around the room, which was bigger, much bigger than the space it seemed to fill from the outside, bigger than the whole building, a puzzle, a string winding like a labyrinth through all things, microscopic and enormous, bigger than any labyrinth ever conceived, and I followed and got lost, had to start over. Another year.

Because that's what it all meant. All it was was time and distance, and what are time and distance but gravity pulling us this way and that, keeping us here, shoving us there, and it all feels the same, whether we're going towards one place or away from another, and people only fit in the crevices. We crash towards each other or away from one another, and it's the same, just a matter of perspective. And that's what all the words were. They were just perspectives meant to keep us tied together like a life raft through the chaos, but the raft was only a figment, useful in painting dreams but not genuine light or darkness, and the words ultimately meant only that, that the boats are not real, that we are who we are or who we aren't, it doesn't matter, but whoever that is it's alone, alone and crashing, careening, sprawling, and alone. Finally I concluded my research when my family pretended to crash into me and I believed them and let them dislodge me from the infinite crevice of that infinite room. But you can never really remove something from infinity.

Needless to say, my words were not allowed on the university's raft. However, I like to think it's a matter of time and distance—not until they award me that doctorate, I don't think I could possibly care less about doctorates anymore, but maybe someday they'll realize, and then my words, then all words, will mean something, and maybe then we can build a raft that will glide through the cosmos with intention. Perspective is only a matter of perspective. I'm sure it can be overcome in favor of Truth, the Absolute through which we're all falling, all grasping through and against instead of with. And why not build of our own falling, our own loneliness, our medium of madness? And I know the perfect place to build such a raft.

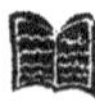

Heavier Things

Carrion House

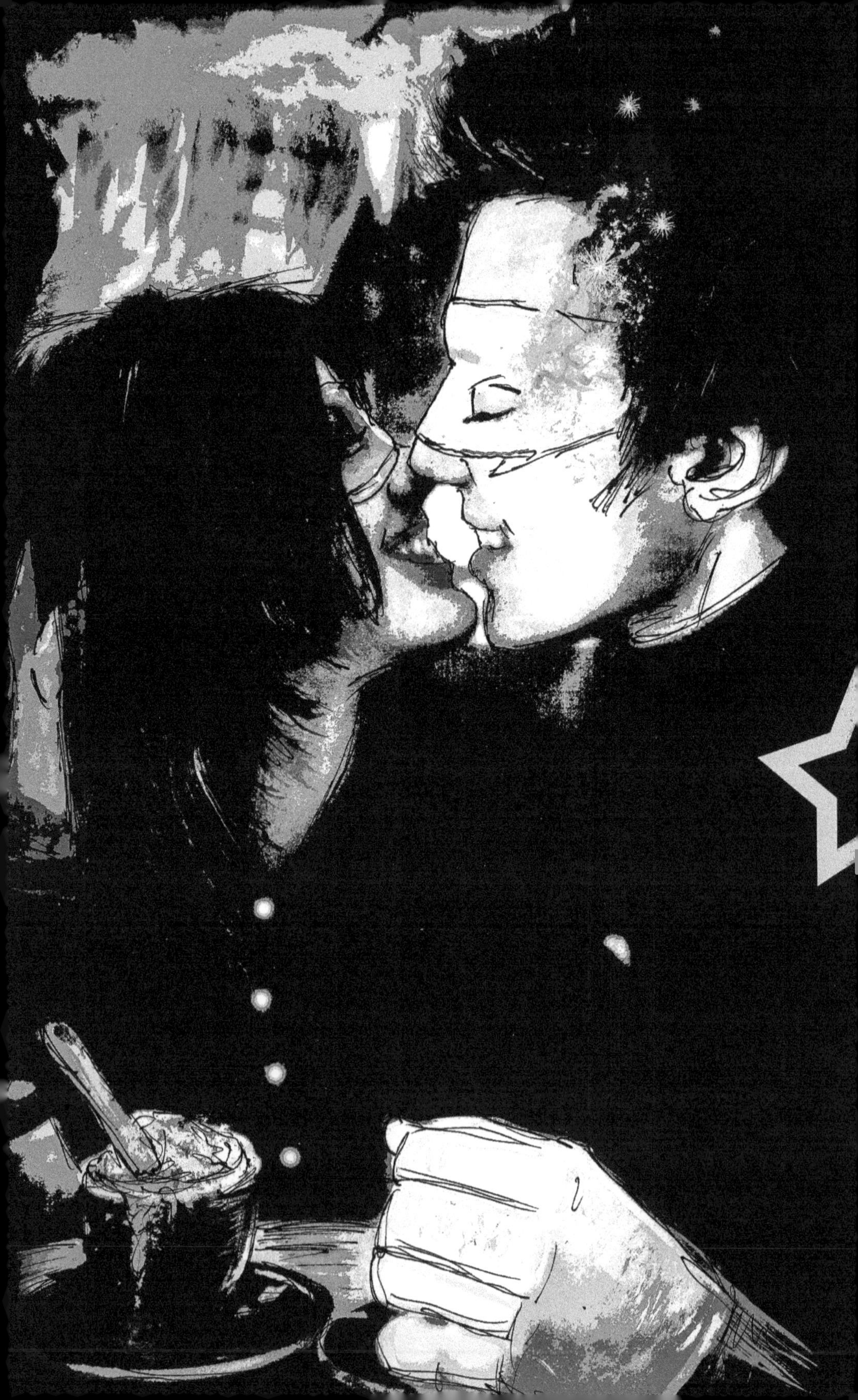

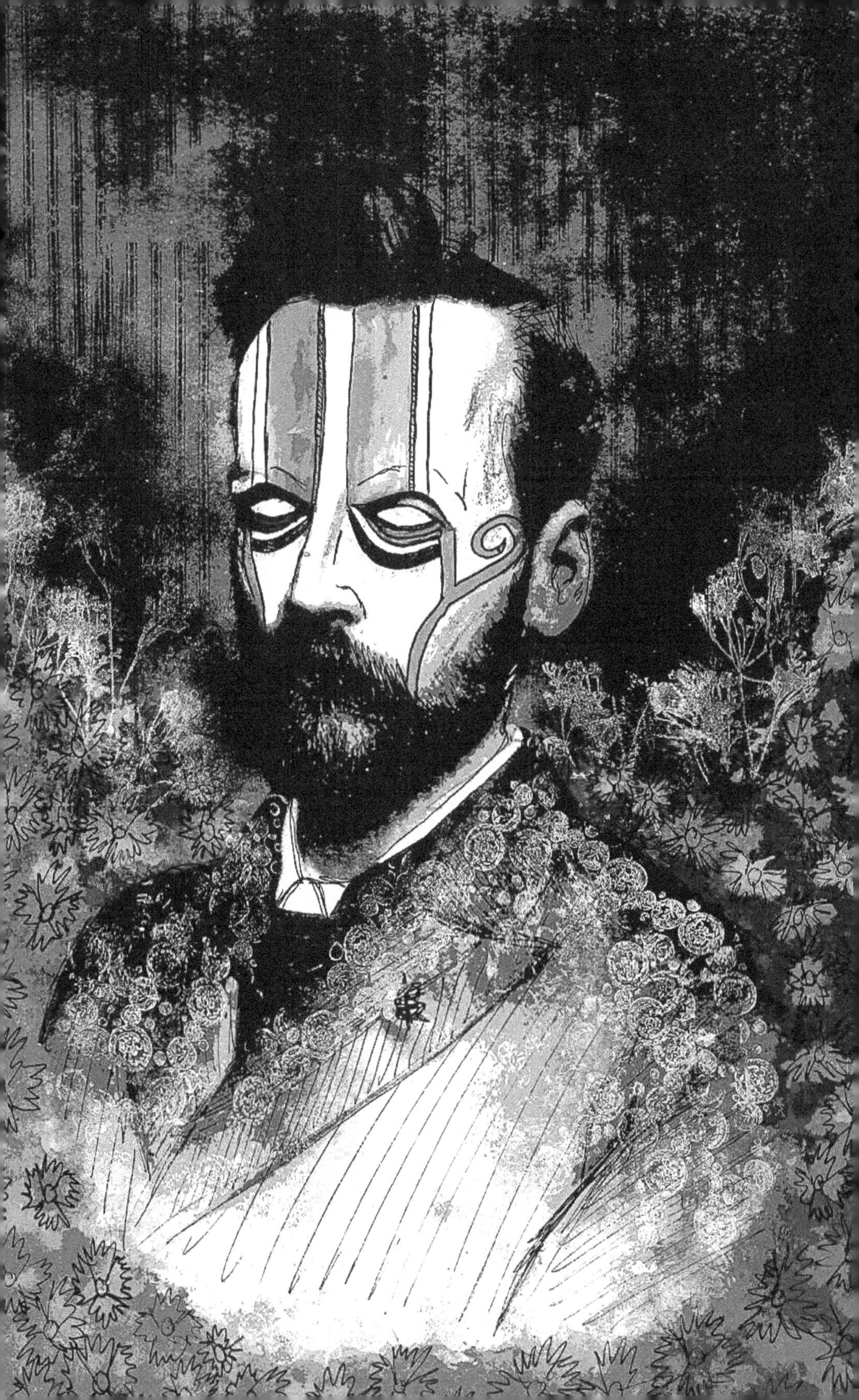

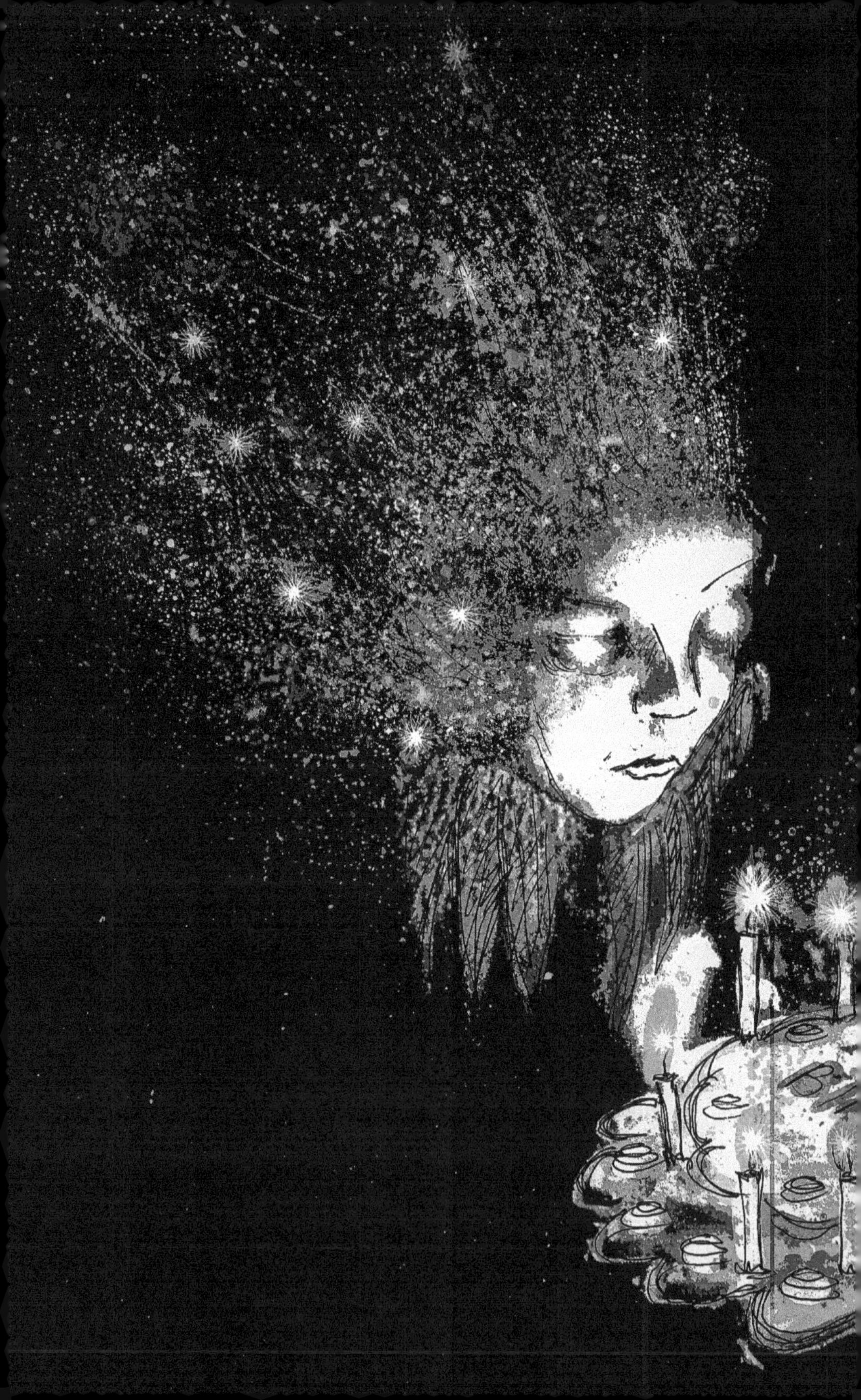

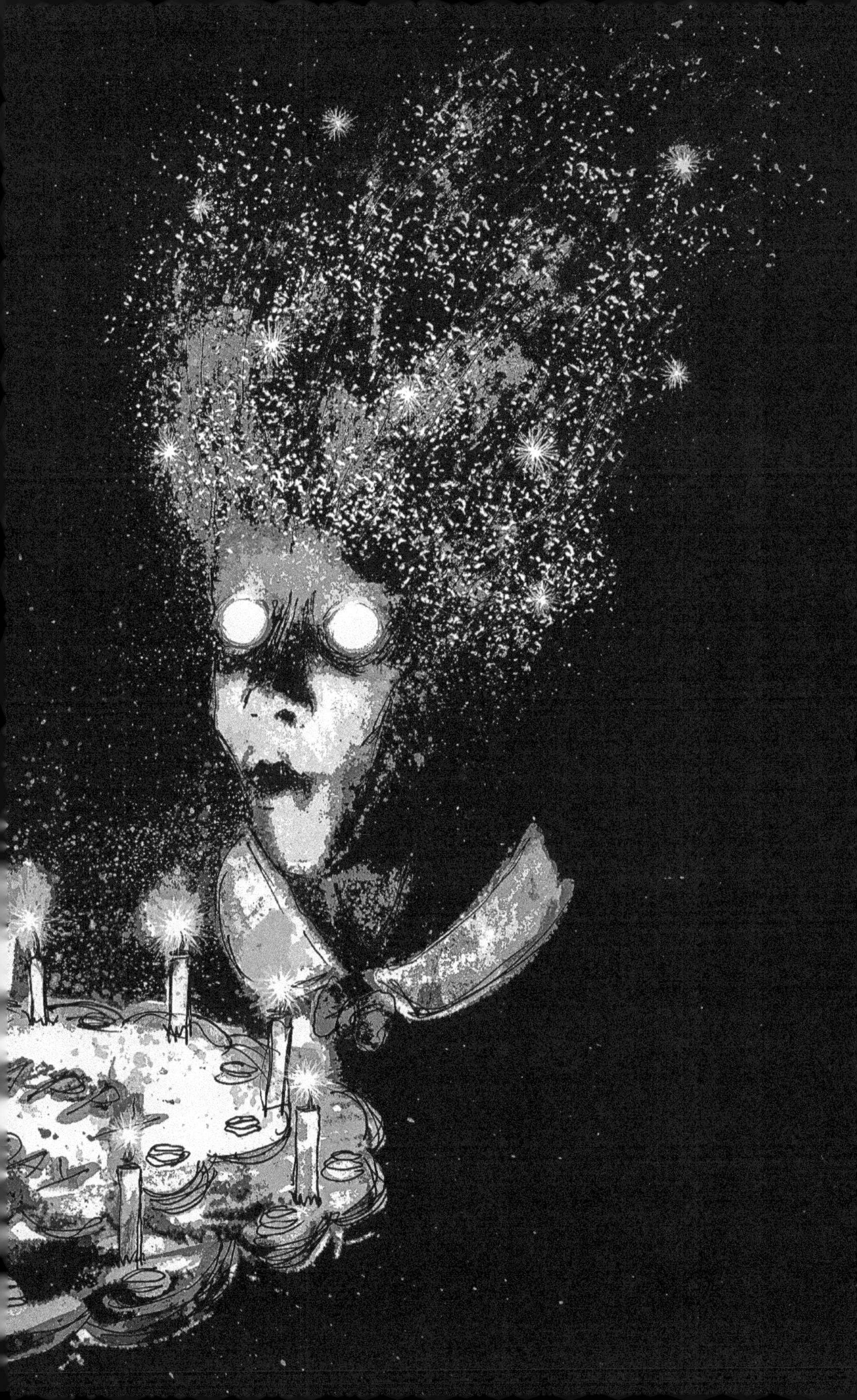

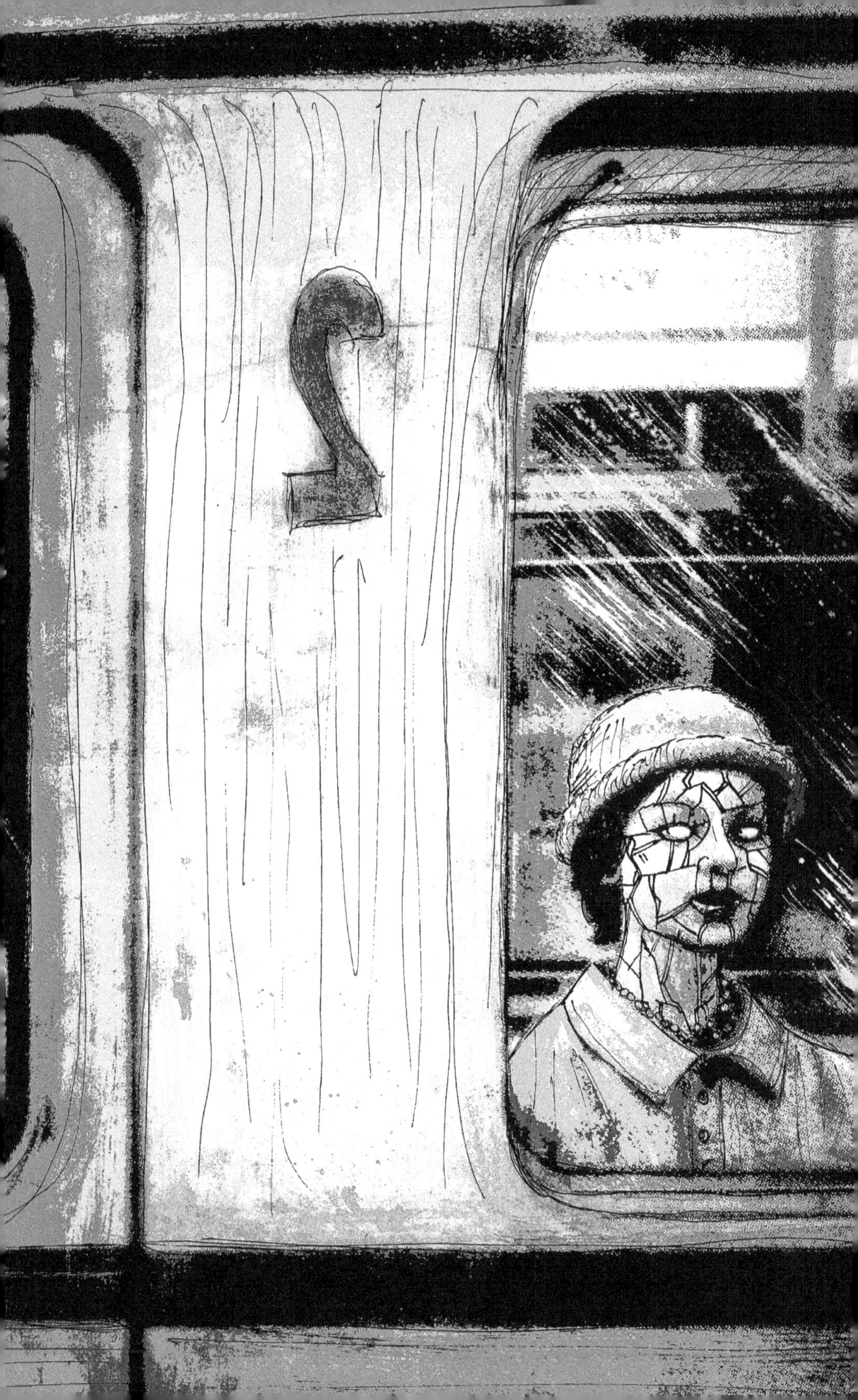

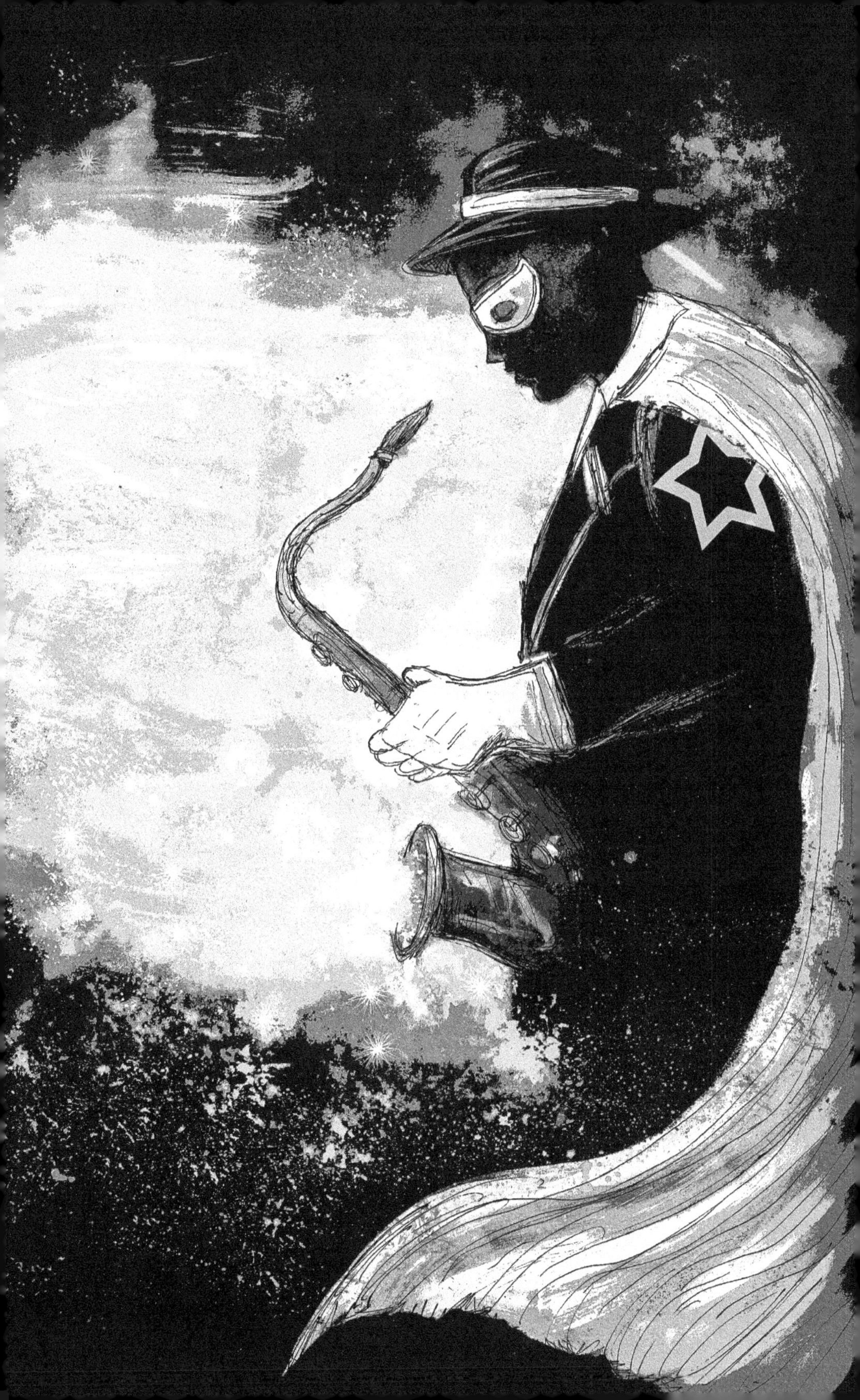

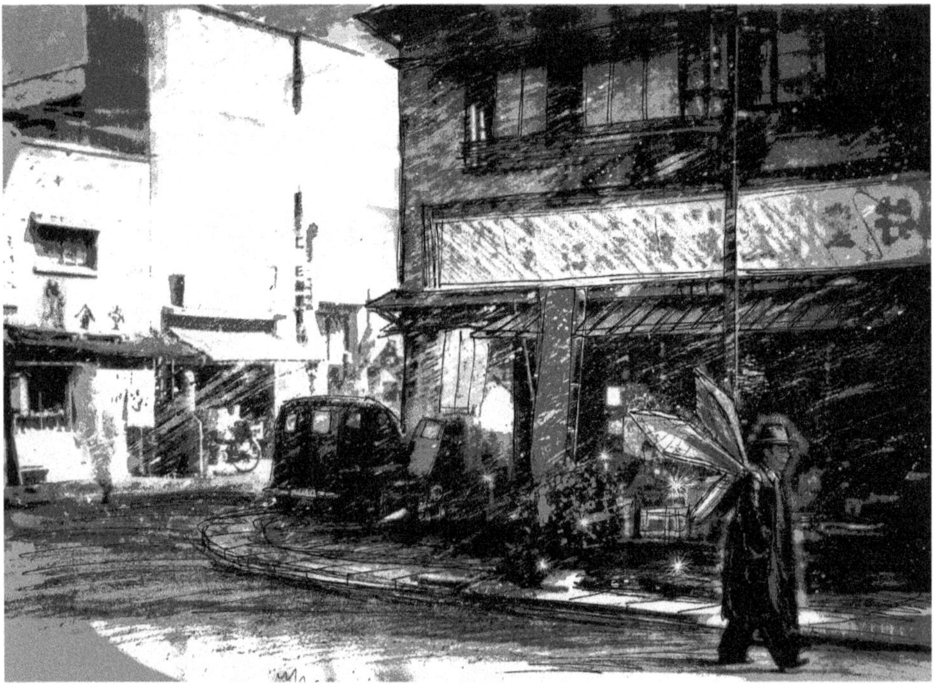

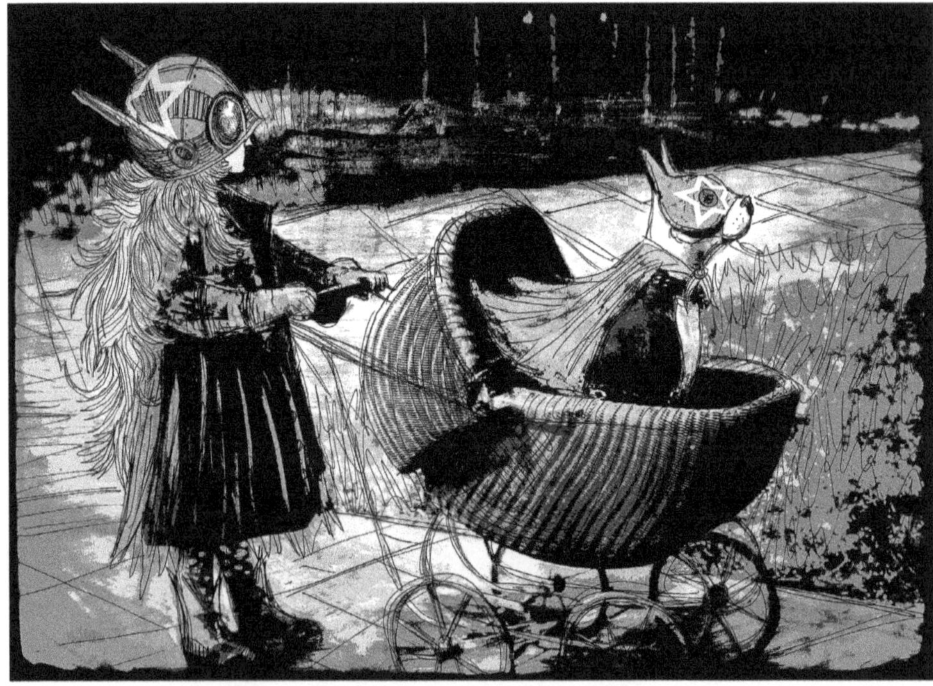

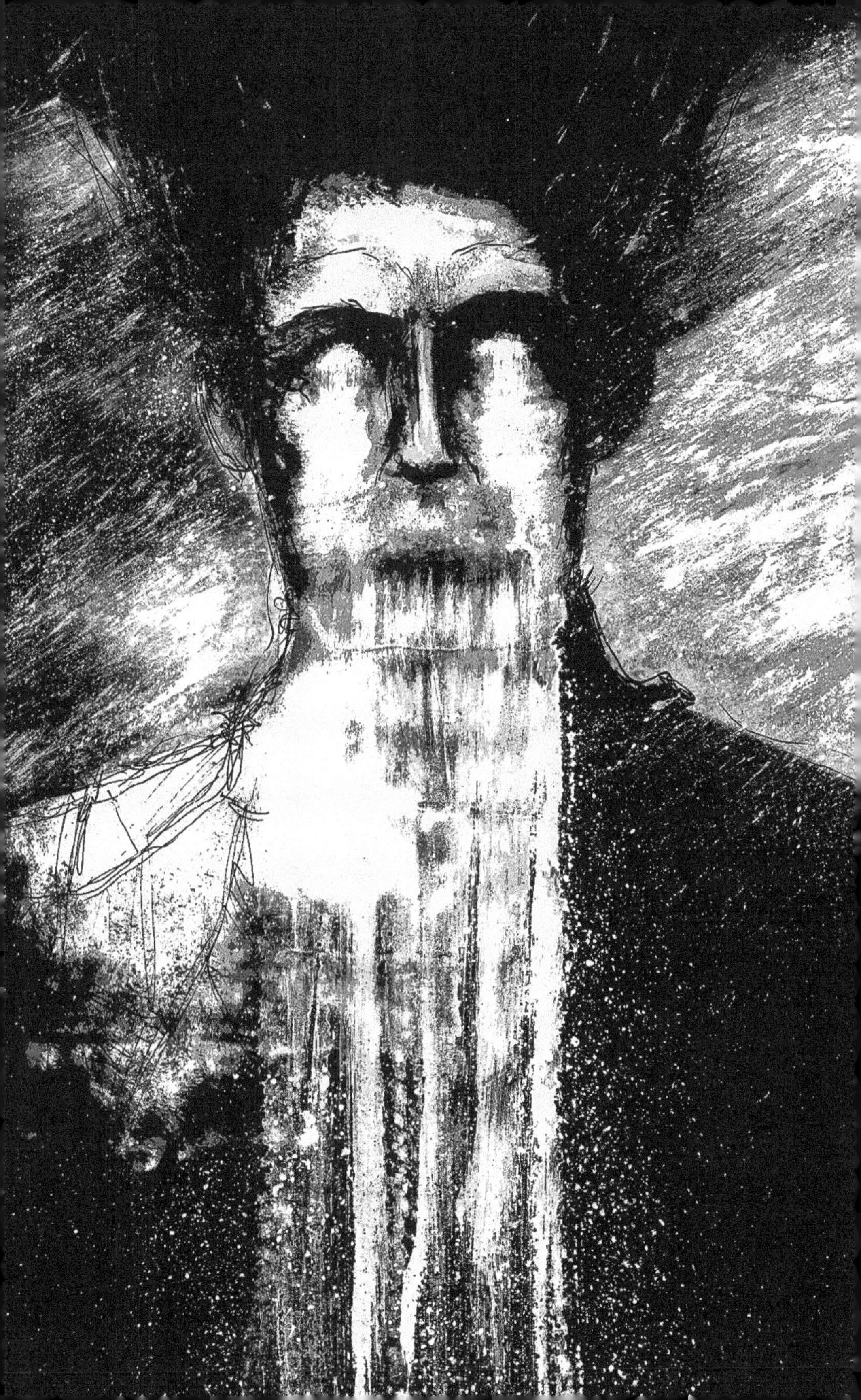

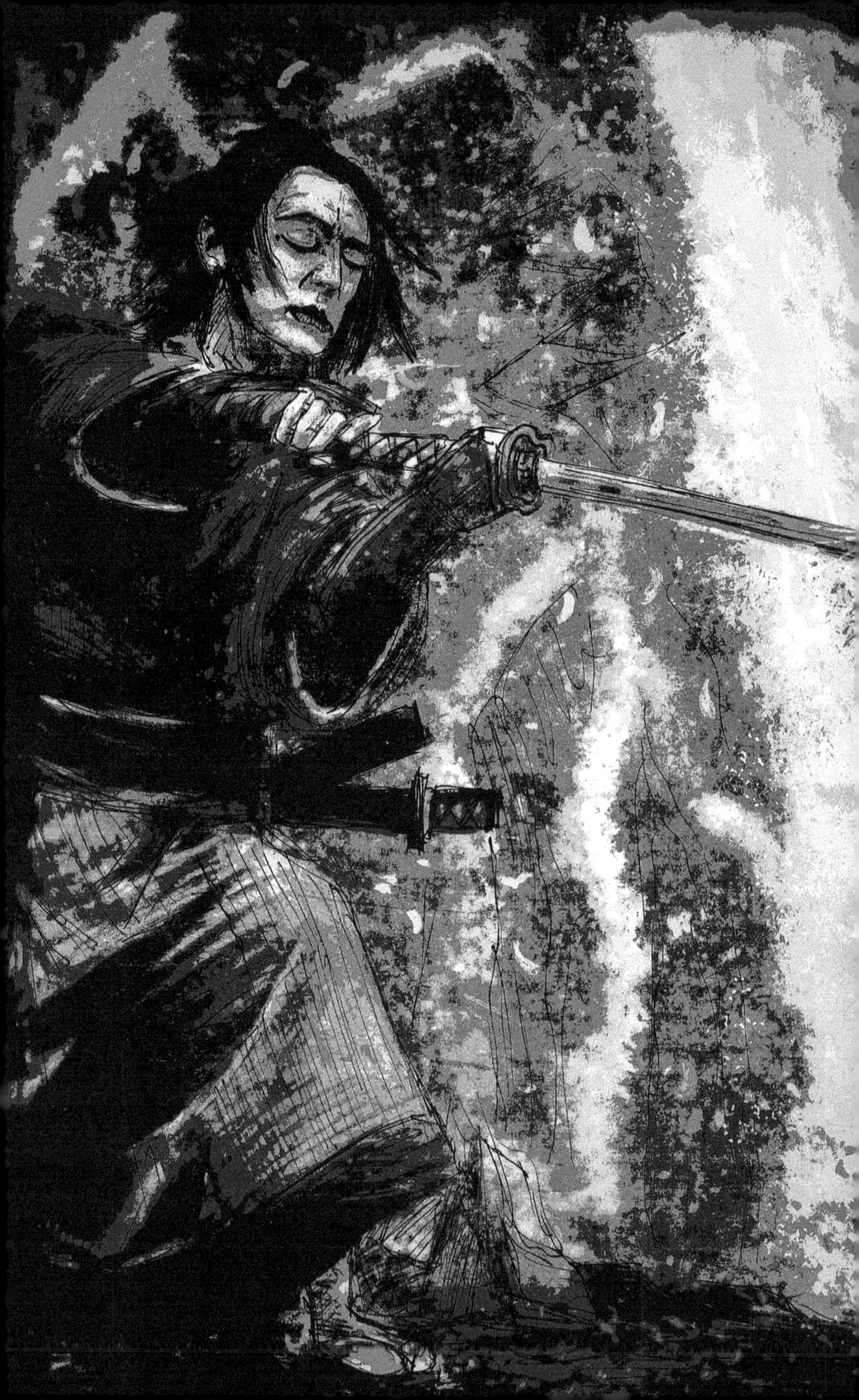

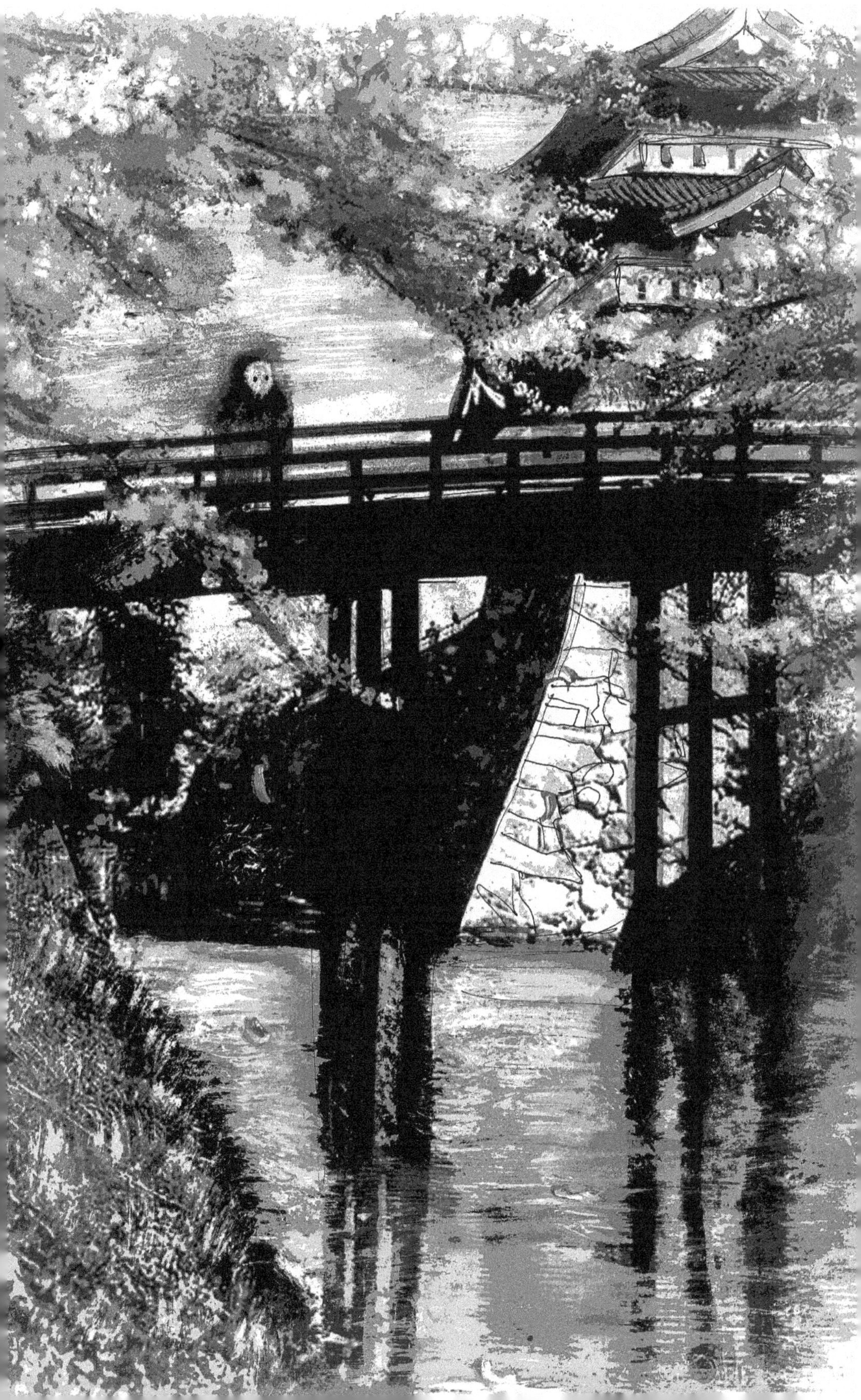

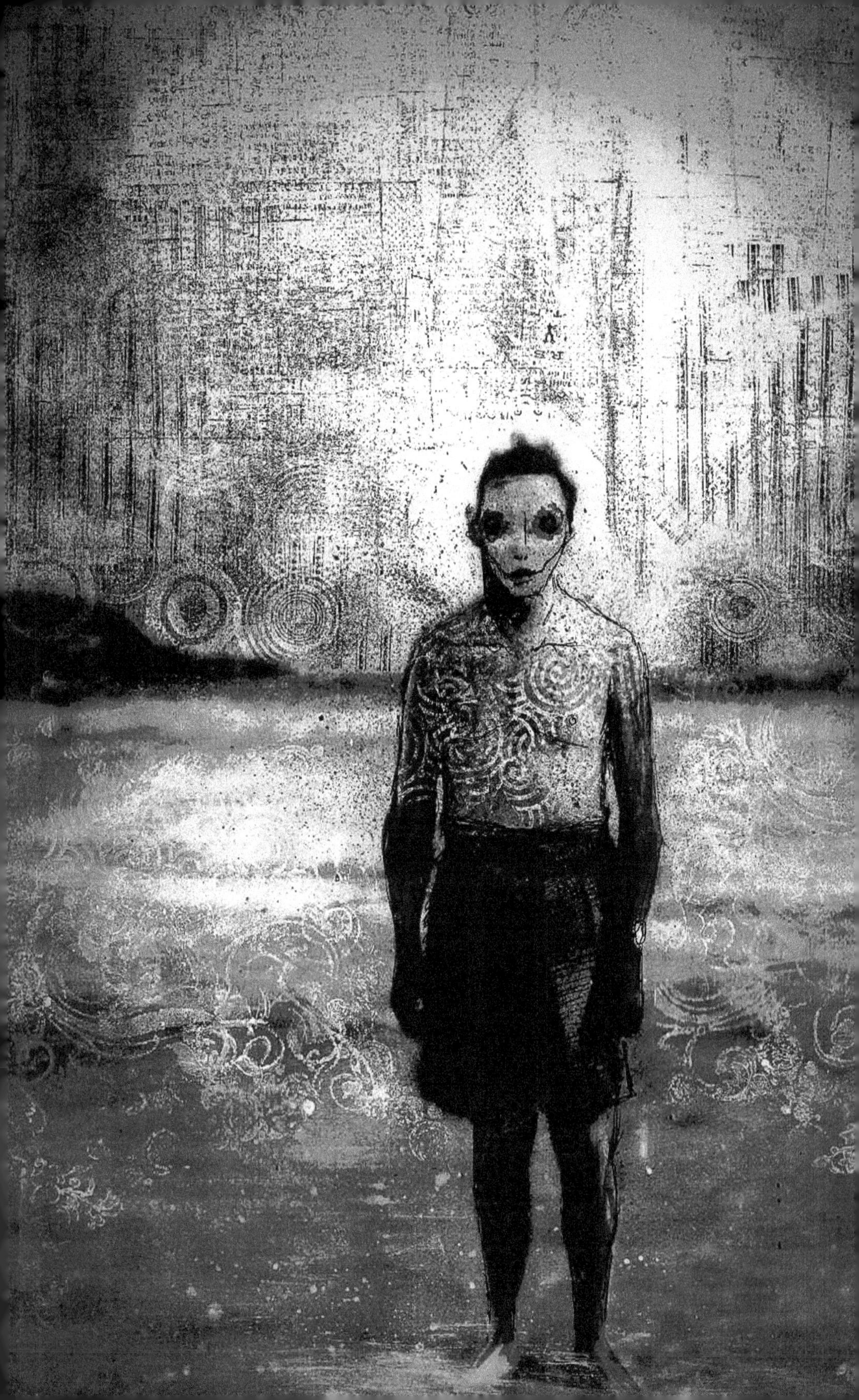

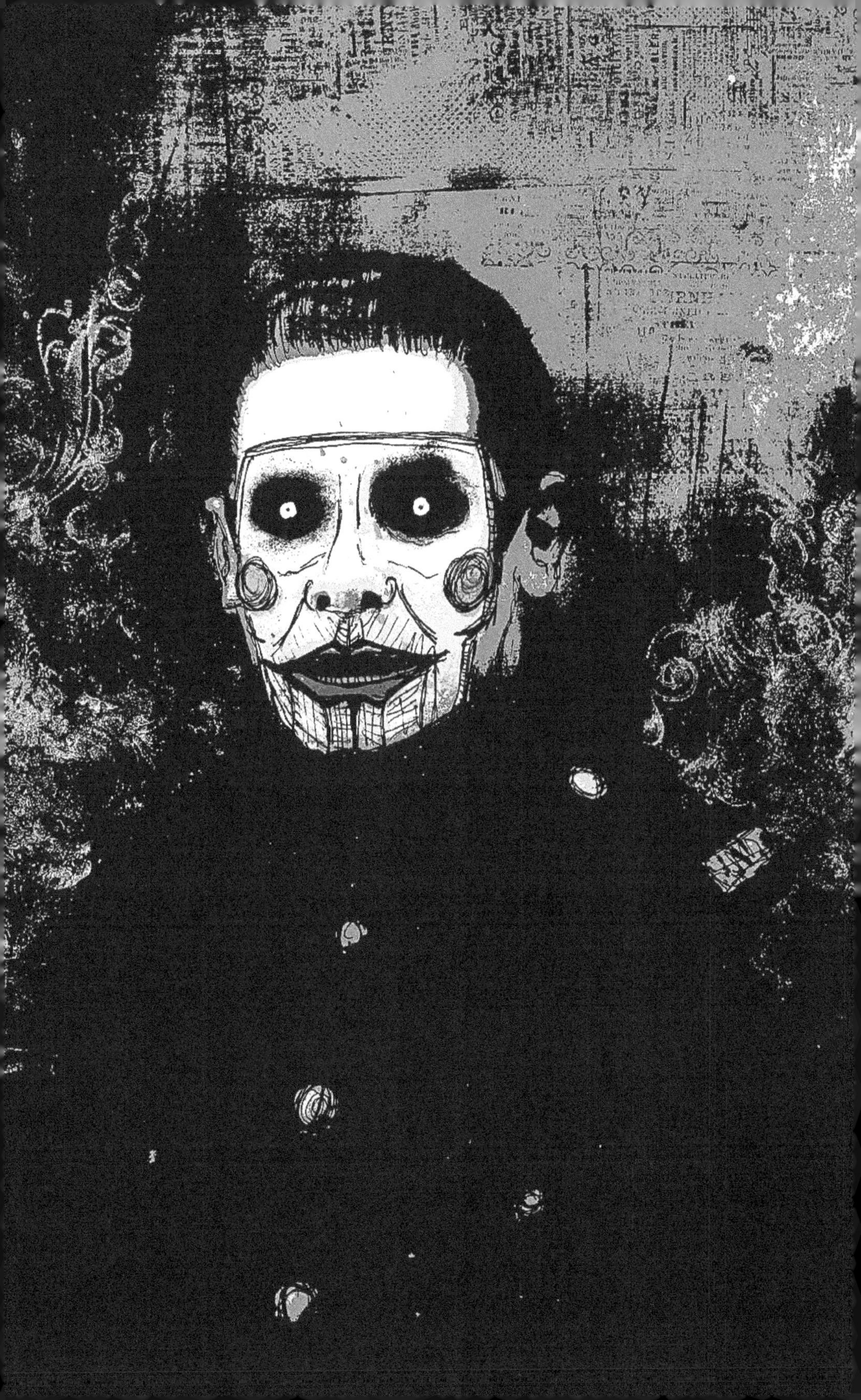

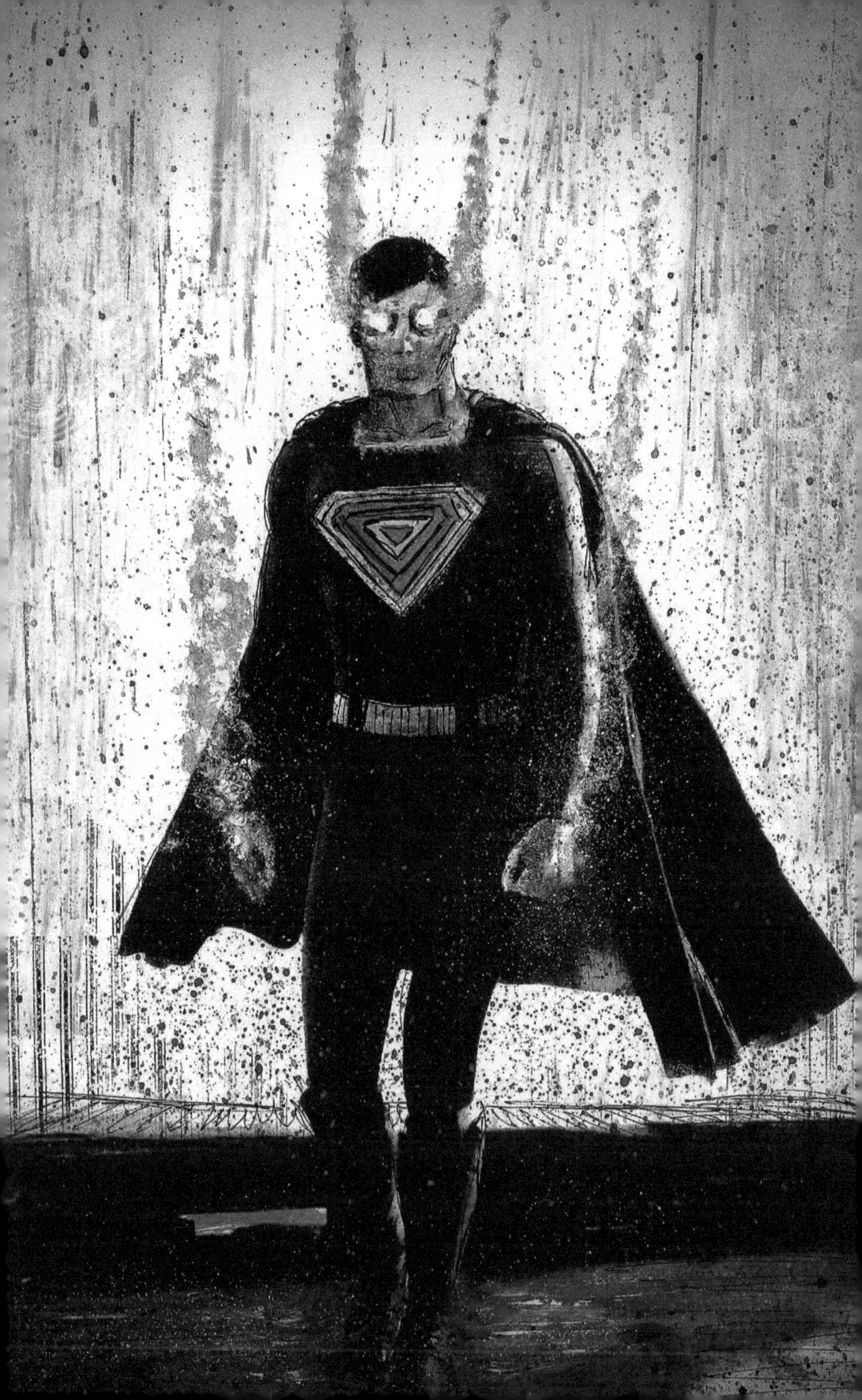

Ms Suburbia

Michele Seminara

What a tame beast she has become, idling
in the paddocks of her family's unmade
beds and mountainous dishes

circumambulating, endlessly, the dead heart
of this domestic poppy field; pausing
with lost purpose to pick up
some   thing   here
and artfully
place   it   there—
in abstract justification
of an involutionary existence.

Look: see how she is
wiping grime from surfaces and
framing frozen memories and
harmonizing dissonance and
feeding feeding feeding

(those who will never be sated)

while deep inside, covertly she is
self restrained by sedatives and
spurred to life by stimulants and
lured to the end of day by the promise
of the darkling hours in which to unfurl
her monstrous might and play—

(what desperate play!)

O what a noble
beast is man
and
O what a cowed
beast is woman—
tethered by the whim
of reproduction
to her most
nominal
self.

Mary

Reymond Drew

I

Mary goes to the car wash in her
Sedan
and never comes home

Mary just sat there in a soap cave
all day long
under attack and nervous

The essence of Mary
is lost to the cloudiness of causticity
the barbarity she must bear, always

until today

when she just evaporated into the concrete
like chemical run-off
the consequences of her
largely ignored

II

Mary swallows four pills daily
in order
to believe that she has
something

Mary slurs her speech sometimes
and spreads her legs
she tells him
to make it quick

Mary wanted to be a princess and
this
is what she
got

Princess Mary gets yelled at for her
superfluous spending
at the Dollar General and
for buying groceries

Mary feels most at peace when there is an
operational
amount
of numbness in her veins

on payday too
when for that
one
morning
hour
at the kitchen table when she
smokes her cigarettes and
pays her bills
she can feel like she has
some
thing.

Hankering

Stefanie Freele

Stephen Jones, M.D. inspected Michaela's scar, while she in return inspected his nametag for the possibility of swallowing it. As the orderlies wheeled her gurney from one room to another, she spied purple latex gloves on a counter and zipped them into her mouth, chewing lightly, just enough to squish them into a wad. Dr. Jones caught this too late and with the help of Annalisa Gonzalez, R.N., wrestled with Michaela's jaw.

Michaela smiled and opened wide. "All gone."

The doctor frowned. "She's headed to surgery anyway." He added loudly to Michaela. "This is the last time we can go in through your stomach Michaela. Do you understand? Laundry detergent, cigarettes, batteries. They can all kill you."

"Anesthesia?" Michaela nodded. "Right on."

Michaela's brother Enzo tugged at his mother's earring before they entered the recovery room. "Ma, when are you going to learn?"

"I forget." She pulled out the other earring, asked the nurse for a safe place to put her purse and looked over to her son. "She was doing so well."

"They lie, remember?" He watched the swinging doors for his sister. "Part of the deal."

***

Nurse Gonzales wheeled Michaela into a corner, away from equipment, hanging posters, thumbtacks, drawers. "She's done. Fine. Groggy. You know the routine."

"Honey?" Ma leaned over and smoothed Michaela's hair.

Michaela's eyes fluttered. "Last time."

Enzo stood back against the wall. "Sure it is."

Without opening her eyes, Michaela spoke in a slur. "Doctor Stephen Jones says last surgery."

Ma stood up stiff, speaking to the nurse, to Enzo, to a doctor, to anyone. "What happens next time she swallows a toothbrush or a spoon and they can't retrieve it through her esophagus?"

Dr. Jones glanced up from the chart. "Too much scar tissue."

Ma pulled at her collar and pinched her son's sweater sleeve toward her.

Enzo shrugged her off, folded his arms and pushed harder against the wall. "Then what? Dirt passes the old fashioned way, but hard items? What about pen caps, wire, staplers?"

They all knew the answer and no one responded. Not even the doctor.

"What about the light bulbs?"

"I really didn't like the light bulbs." Michaela murmured.

"Oh good sweetie." Ma smiled at everyone. "That's such terrific news."

"I'm so tired of this." Michaela whispered.

"Good sign," said Dr. Jones as he looked into Michaela's eyes with a small pen light and repeated toward Michaela's mother. "Good sign she's getting tired of it."

Ma hugged her son's folded arm. "Maybe this is it. Maybe she's done." She squeezed while Enzo flexed his muscle. "Thank you, Doctor…" She scanned his white jacket. "Sorry, what was your name?"

The doctor glanced down at his chest then sharply at Michaela who lay still like a closed-eyed Mona Lisa with just the slightest smile on her face.

Still, She Rises

Jessica Hoard

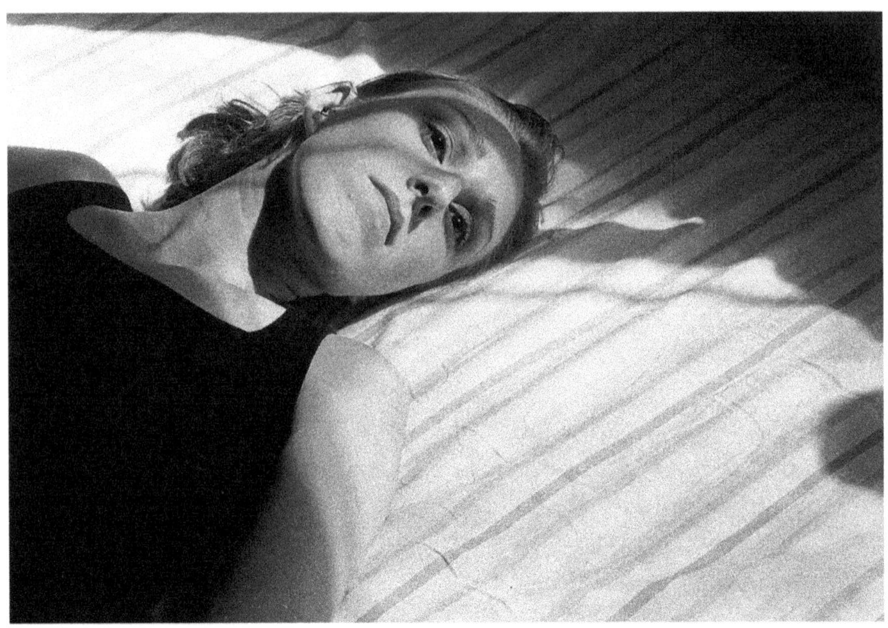

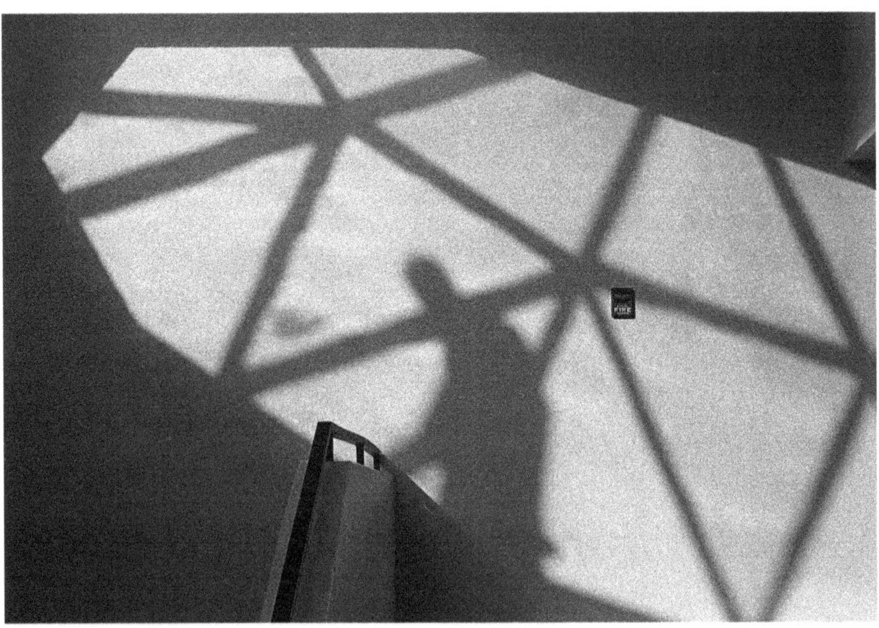

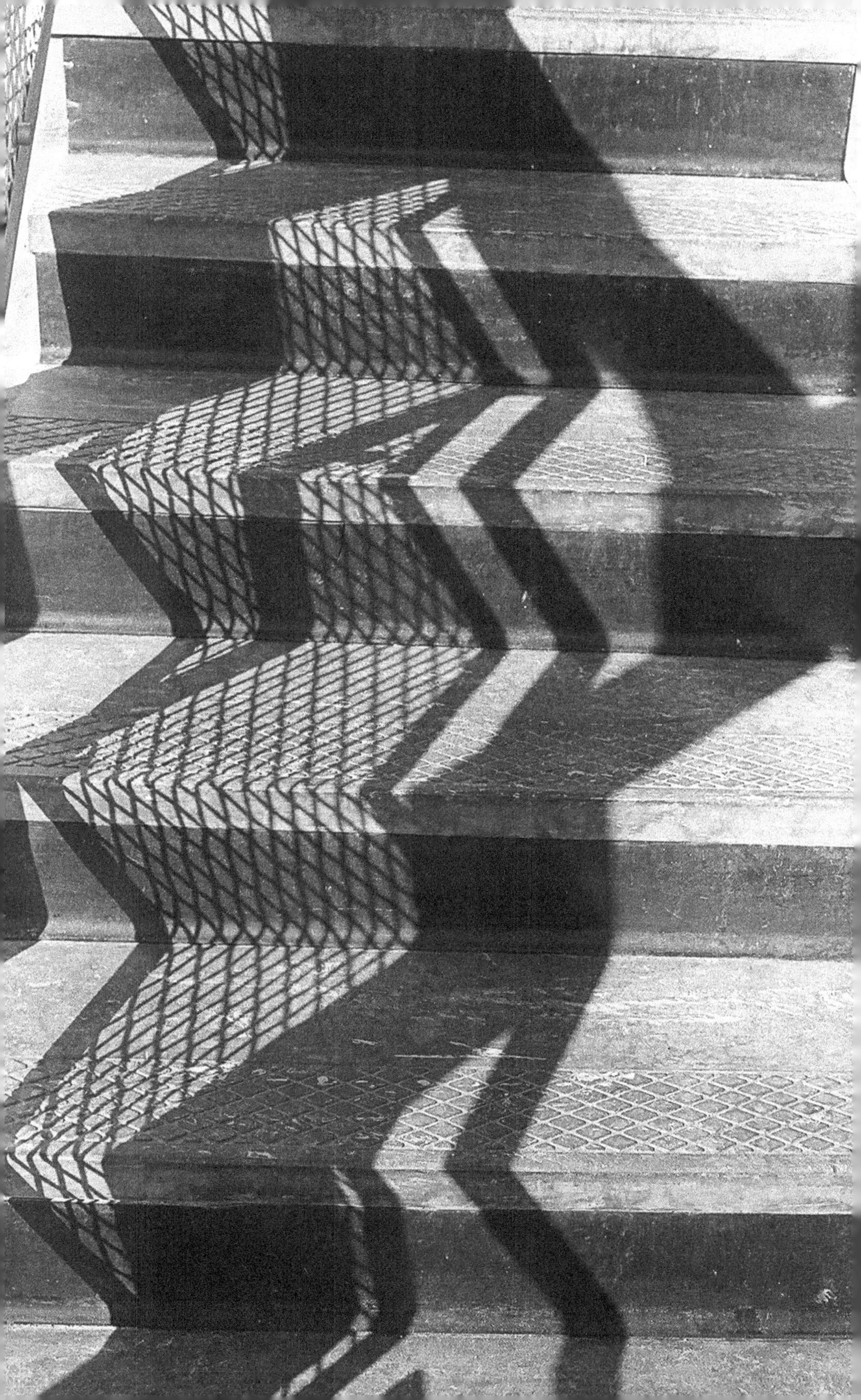

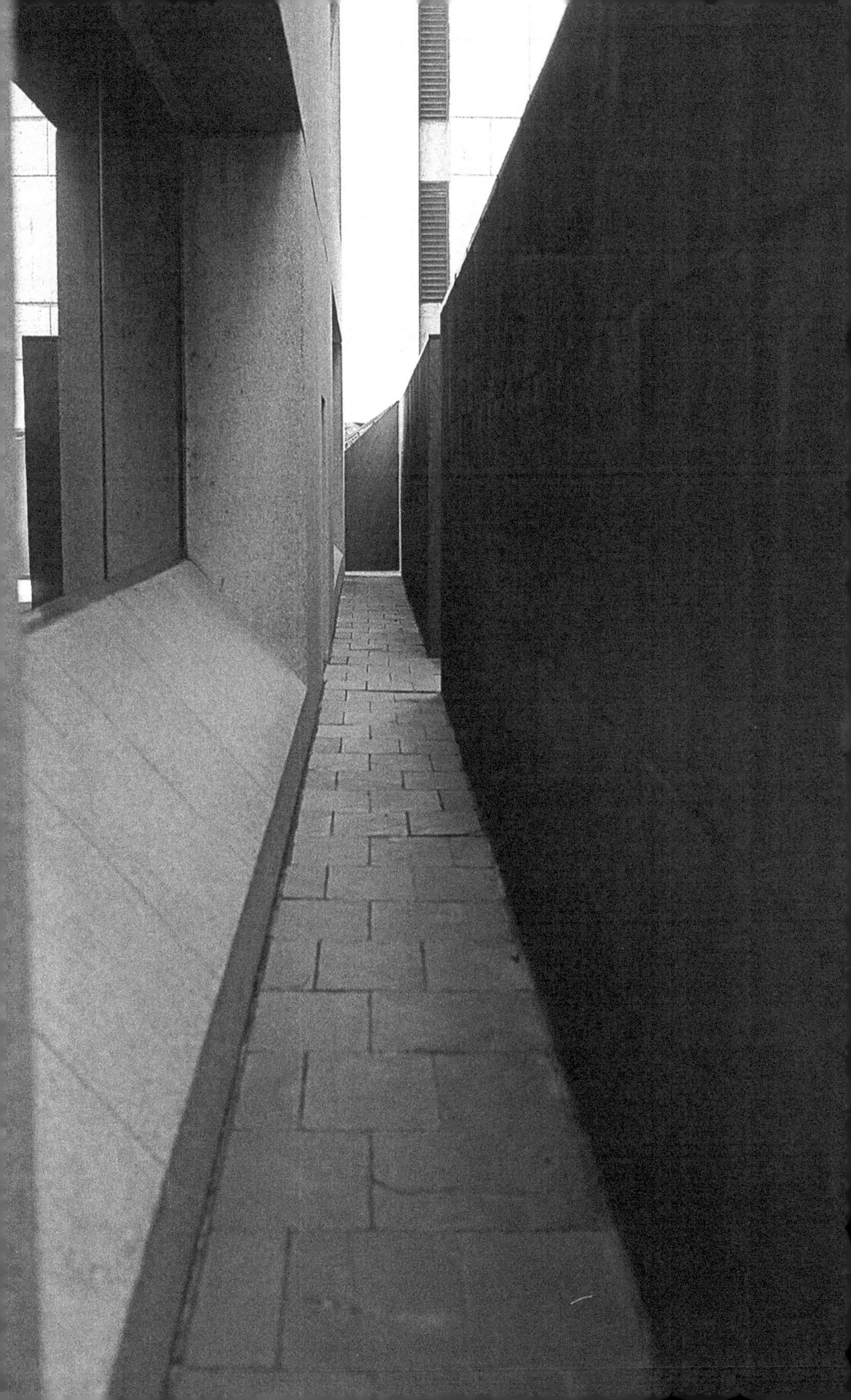

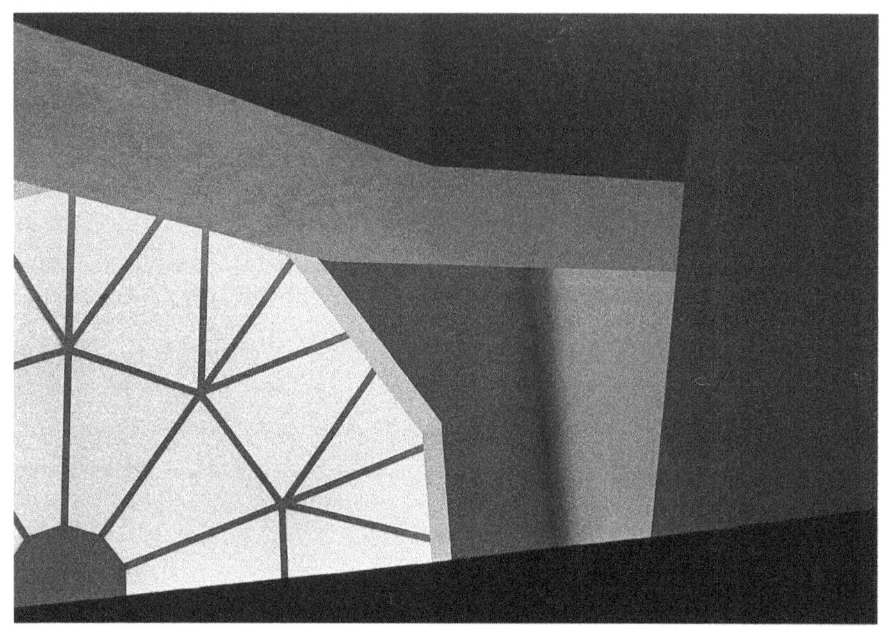

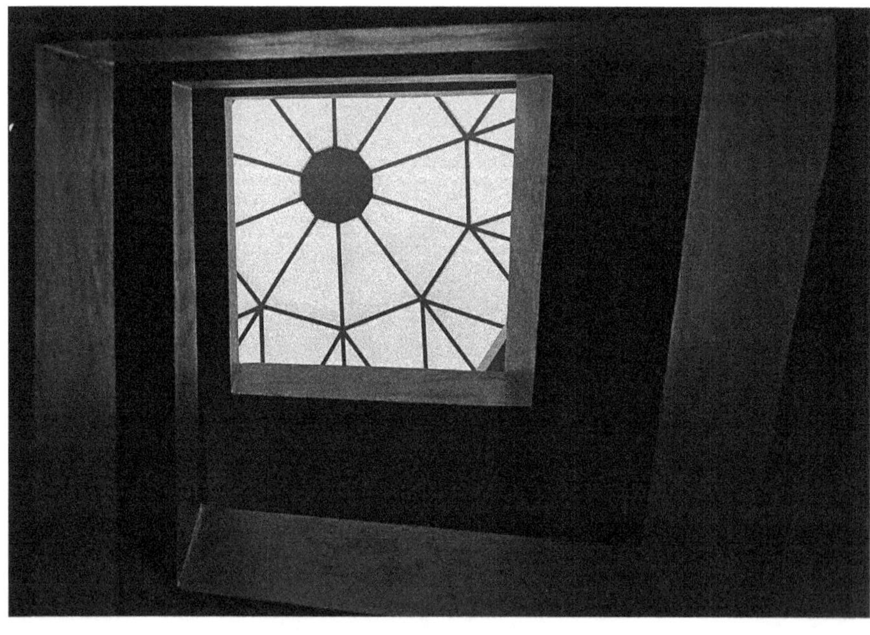

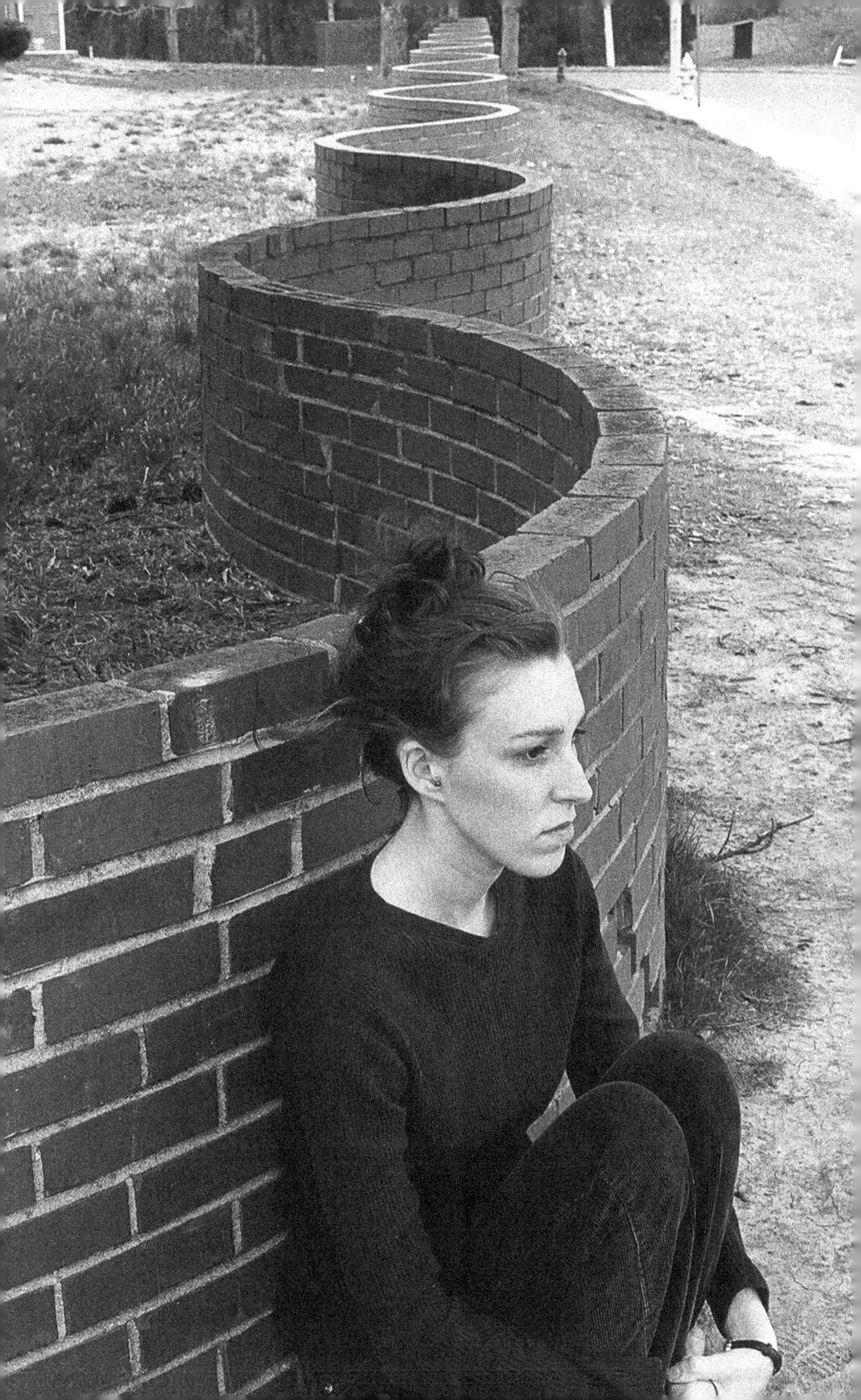

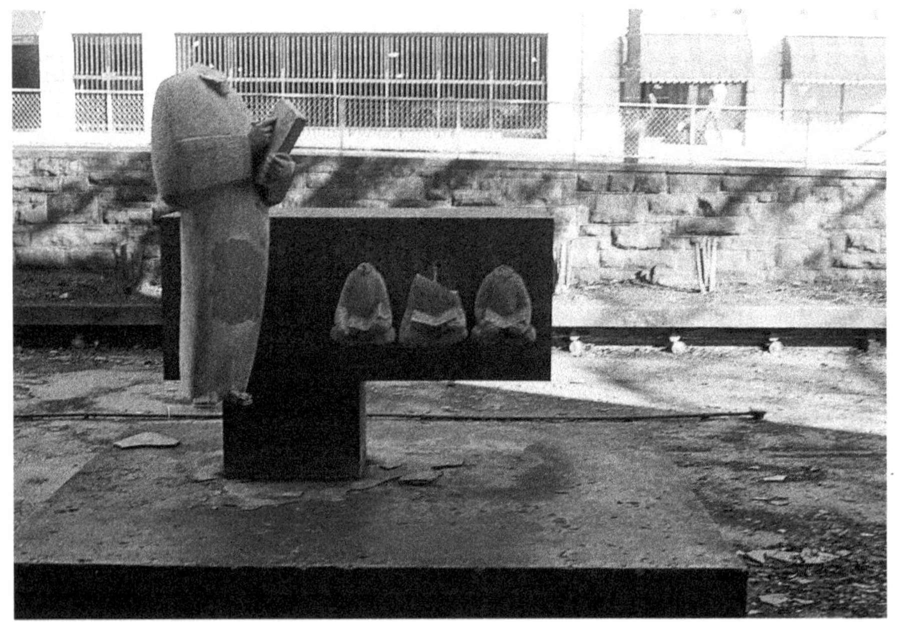

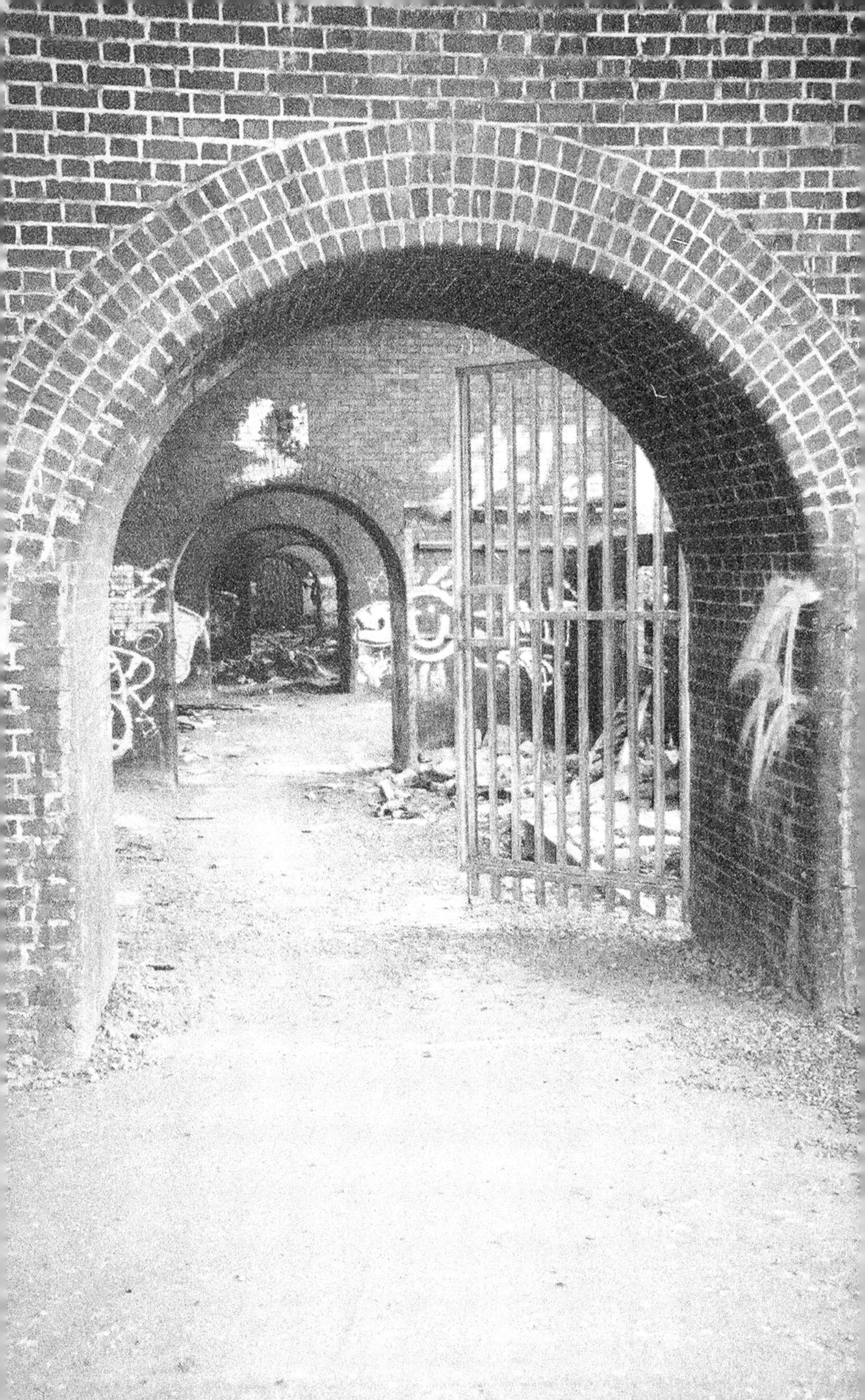

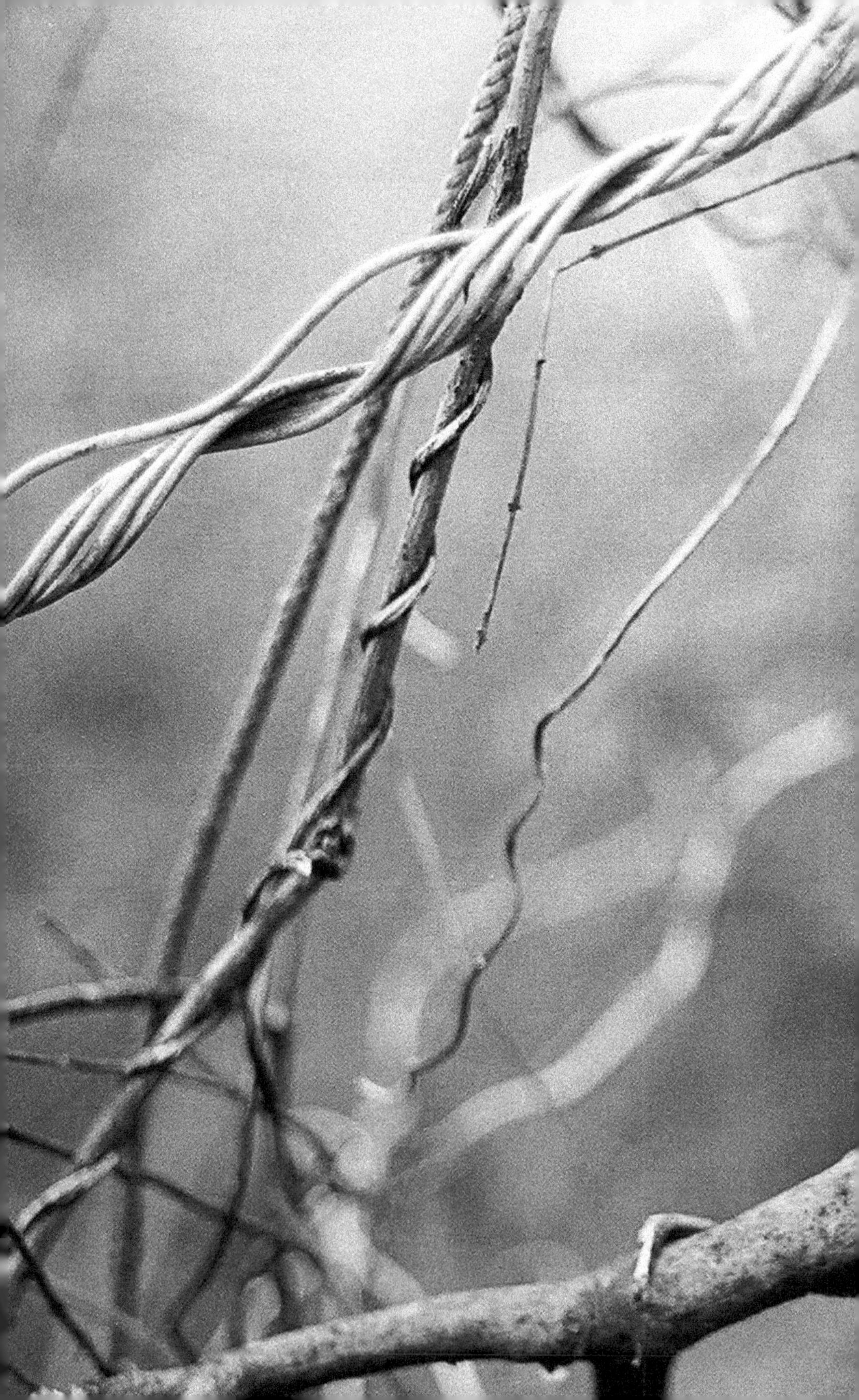

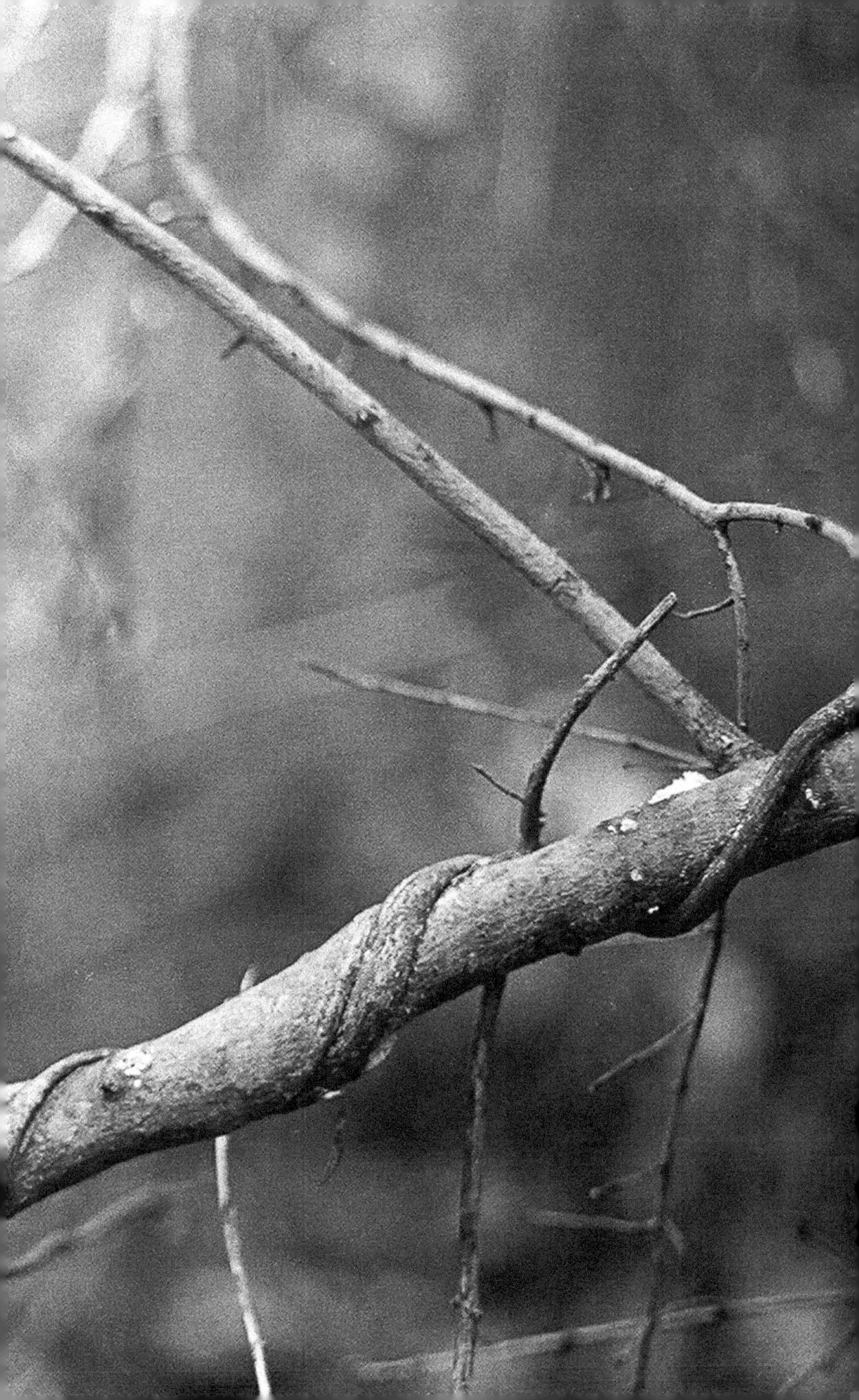

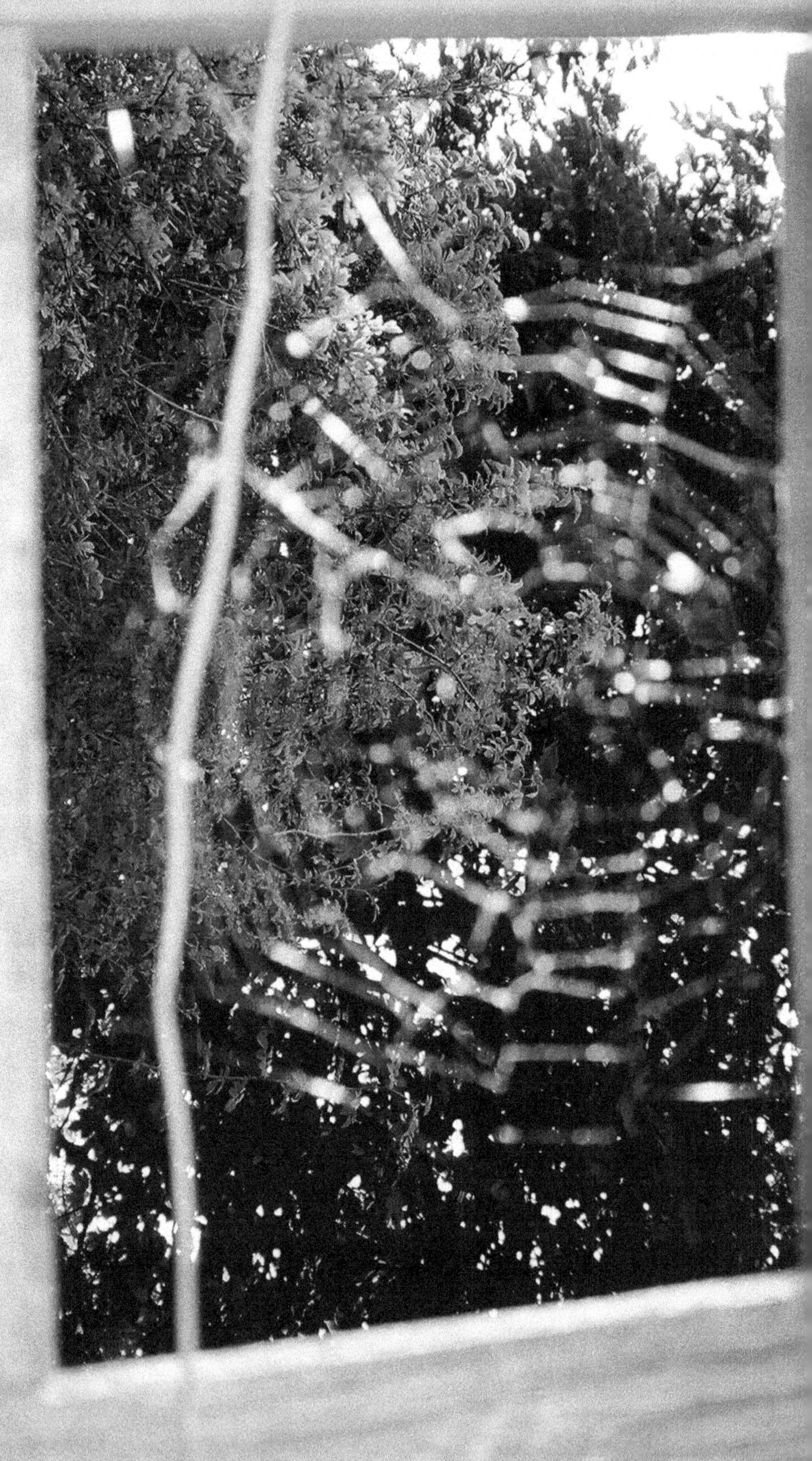

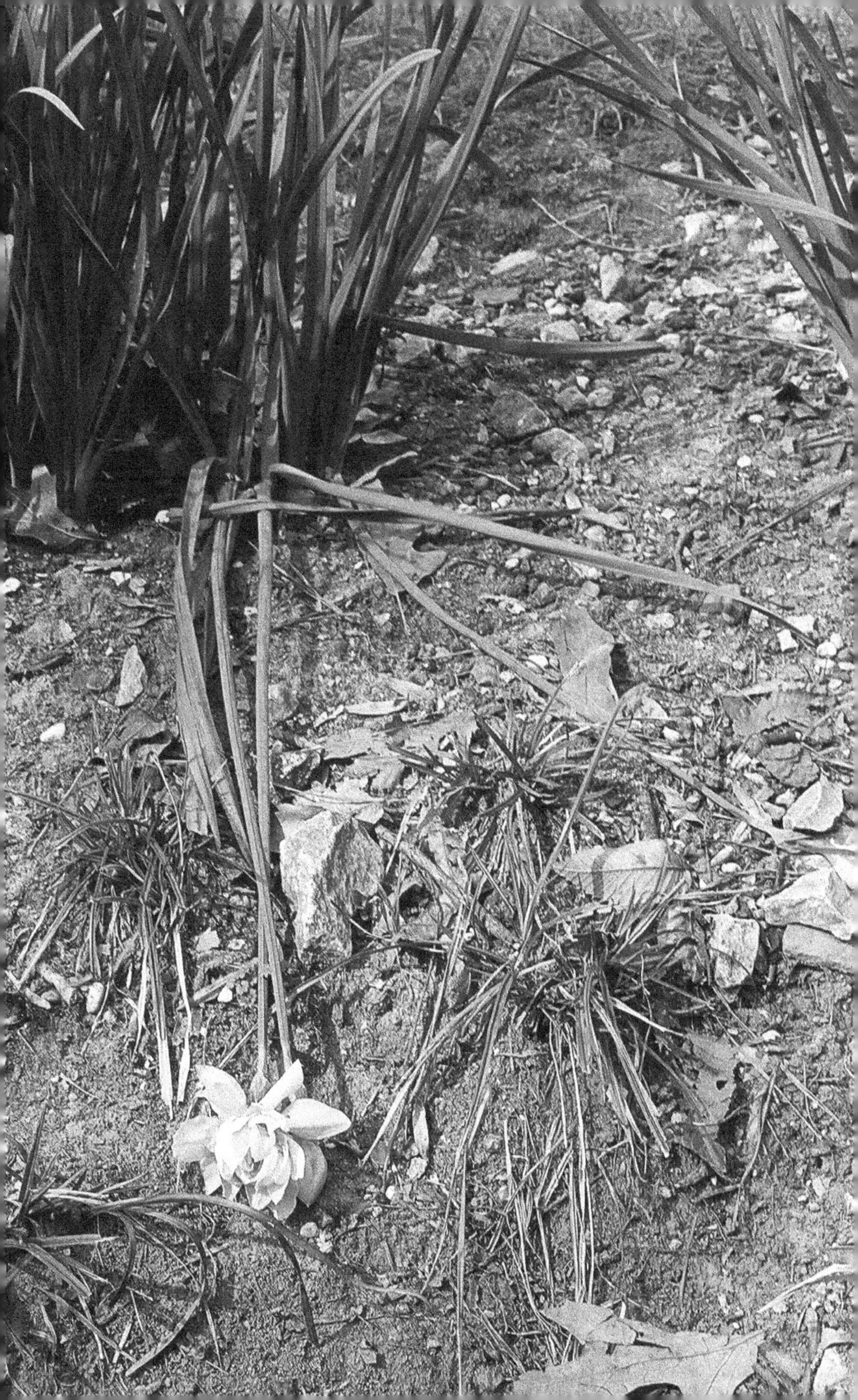

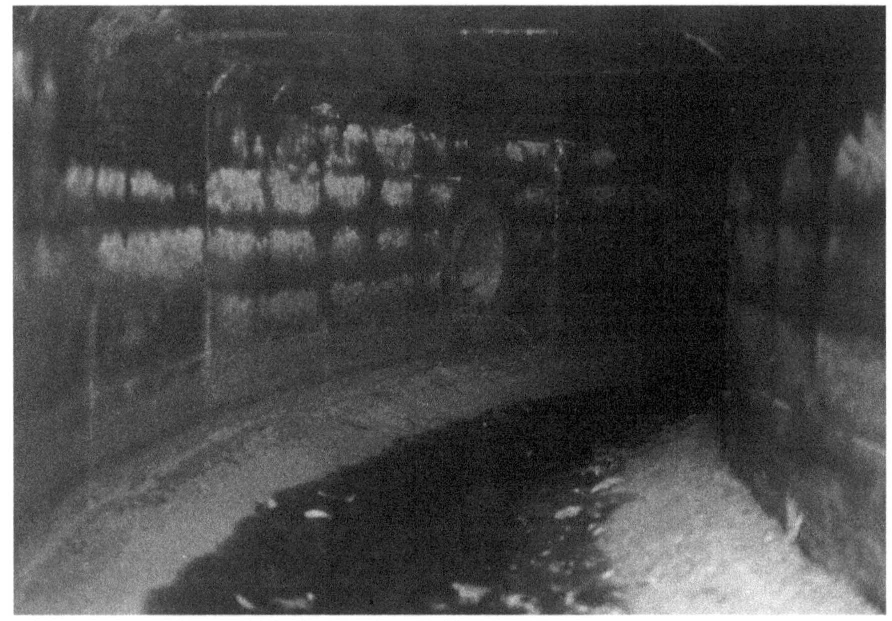

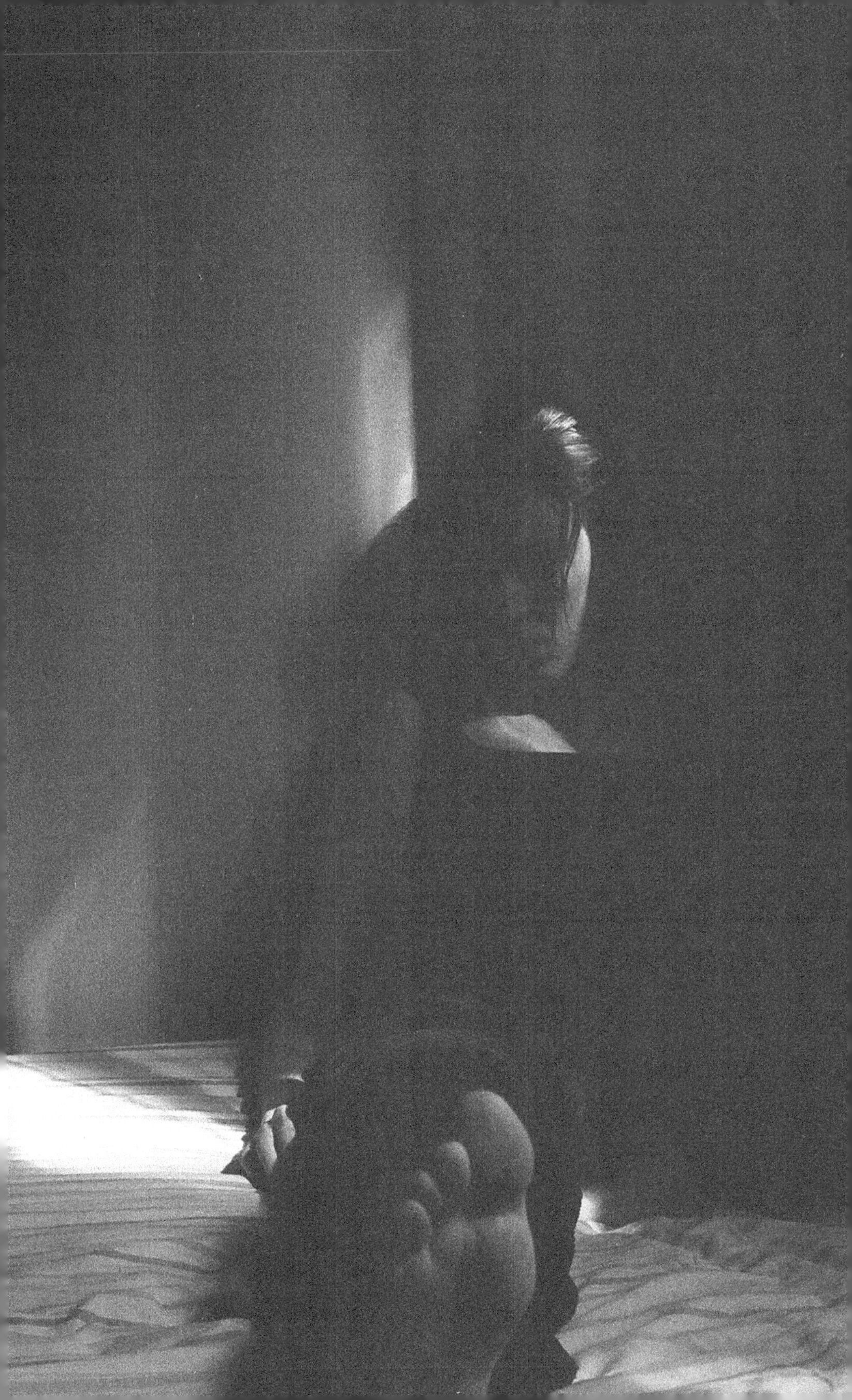

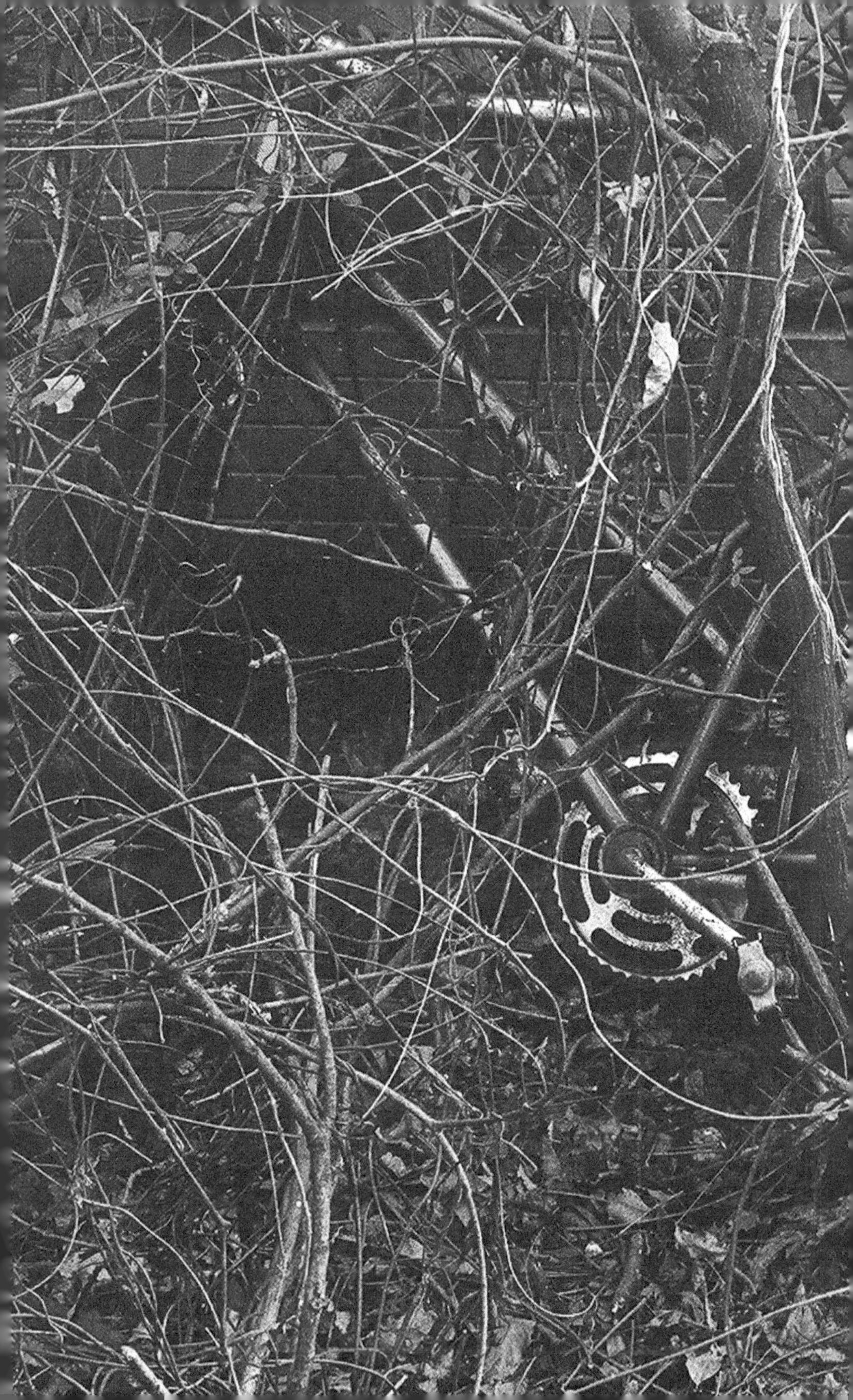

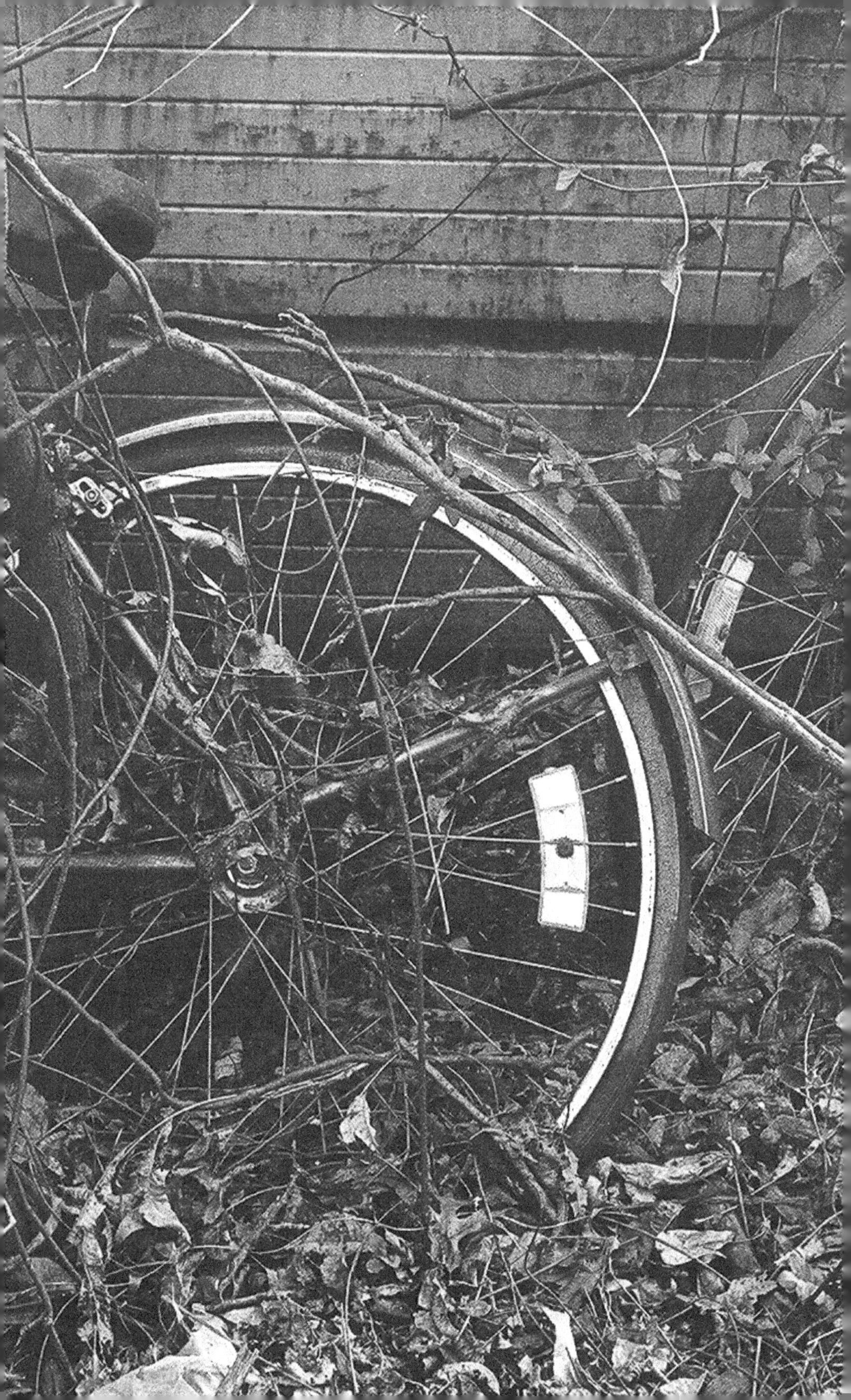

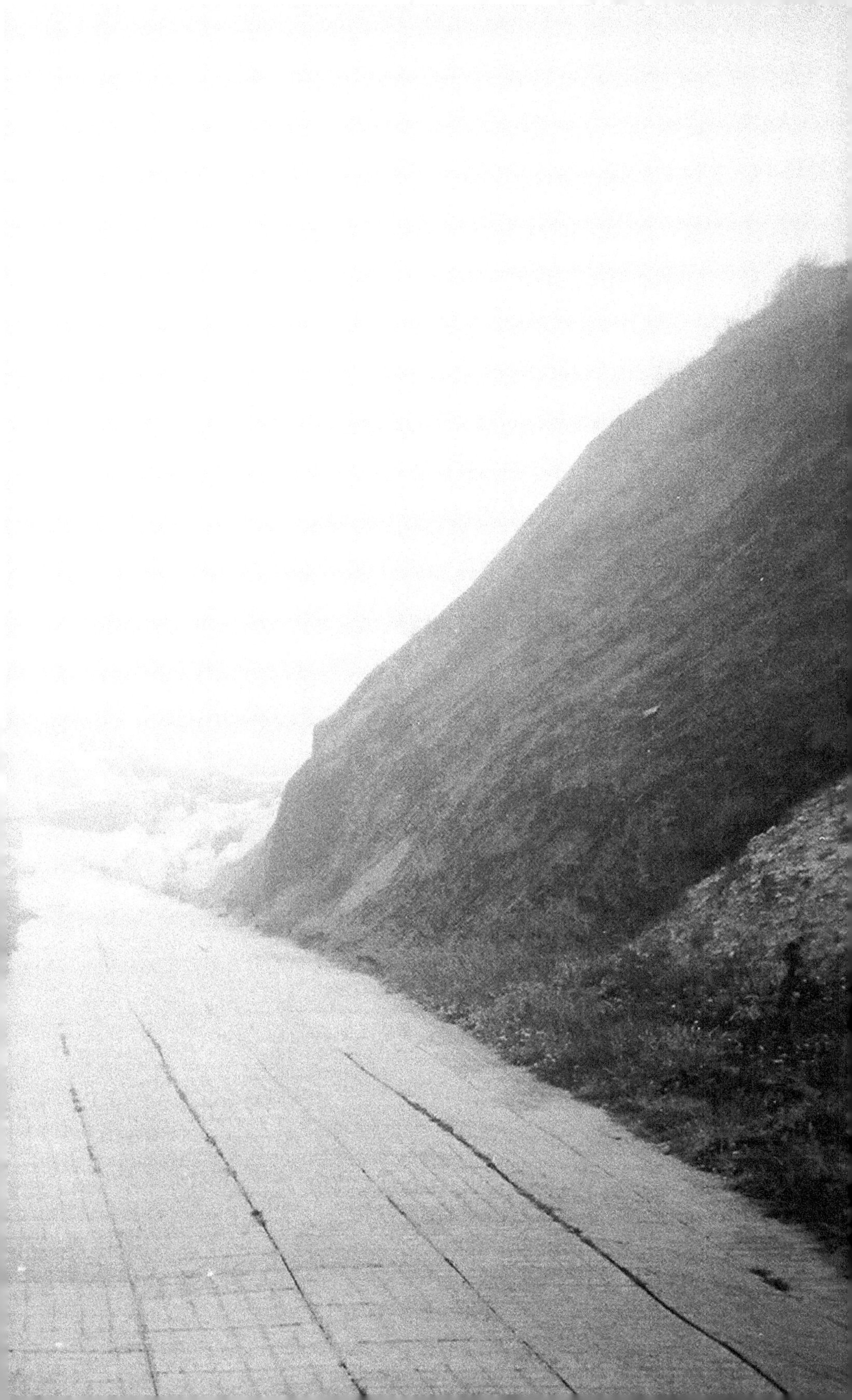

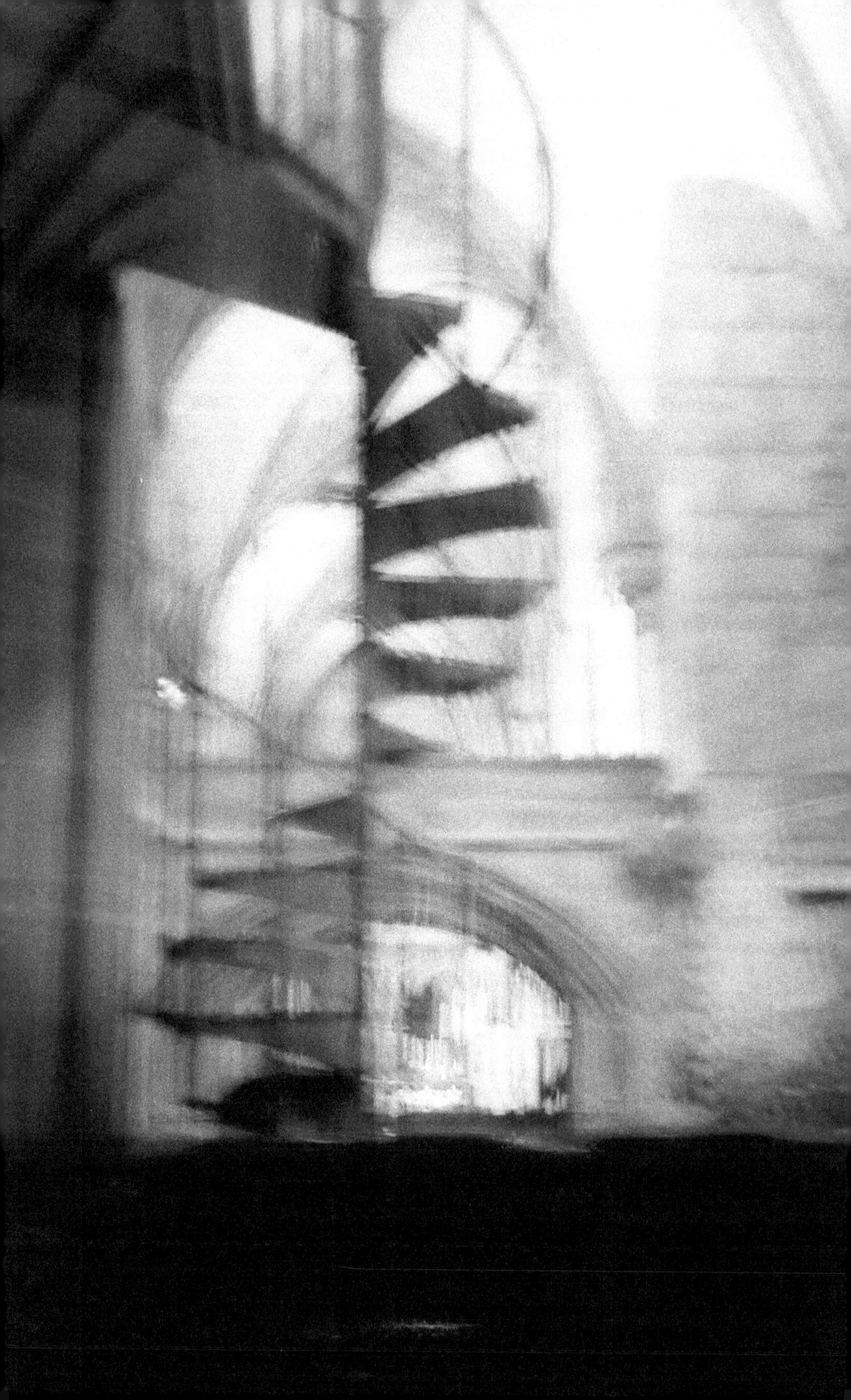

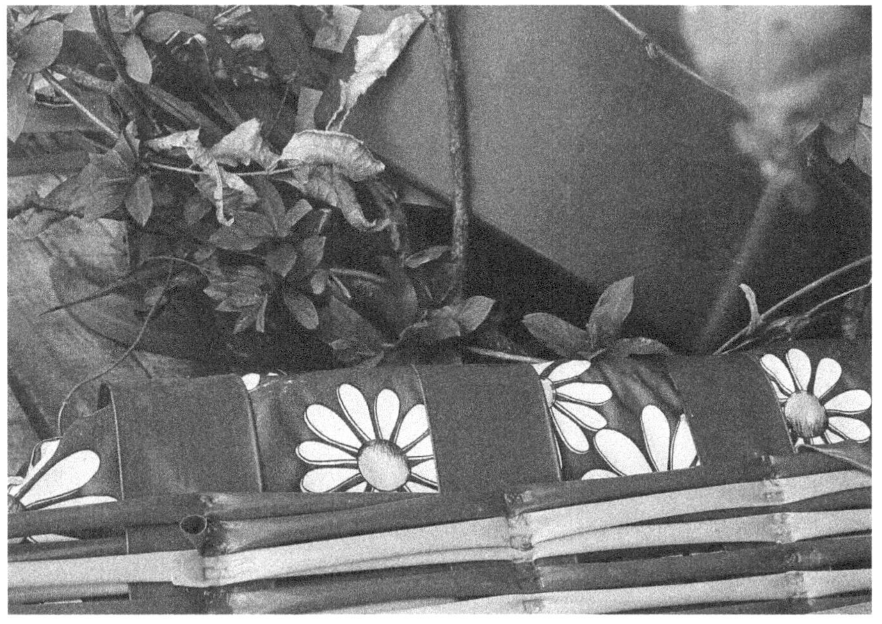

The Three Chagalls

John Vicary

They appeared outside Jane's office at three minutes to eight. Jane recognized Them immediately, even though They'd never been introduced. An observant person would notice the smallest twitch of her right fingers before she reined in the instinct to shake hands and instead quelled the digits into quiescence. "Hello!" she said, betraying her frazzled nerves.

They swayed, but said nothing.

"Oh!" Jane reached for her translator and snapped the collar around her throat. She made sure the transducer fitted snugly against her vocal cords as she pulled the headset forward into her ear. "Pardon me," she said again, smiling. "I didn't realize the time. I'm Dr. Jane Hysell. I'm very pleased to meet you."

The form on the right fluttered. "Doctor. I am ______, and this is __ ______. We are here about the Chagall.

Jane nodded to cover her anxiety. She still wasn't used to the sound of the foreign syllables in her ear. Their names were untranslatable. Even the most recent updates to the software couldn't give an approximation of names, although it did a nice job of bridging the language barrier otherwise. Jane had heard stories from her grandparents' generation when The Occupancy had first taken place, and it sounded like a confusing time for everyone involved. She was glad that they had evolved into a stable society, even if she didn't have much personal experience working with Them. Everyone would learn, she had been told, and this was her chance. "Of course. Right this way."

They followed her through the halls, and Jane talked to fill the awkward silence that was punctuated only by her lone pumps clicking on the tile. “May I ask why you are interested in Chagall? We have an extensive collection of Monet’s work.”

“Impressionism is not an example of the complexity of thought that is exemplified by the Cubists,” __ _____ said.

“Or the Surrealists,” _____ offered. “We are interested in the surreal.”

Jane made a left at the Modernist wing. “We are proud to be in possession of a Dali, if you would care to examine it, as well.”

“Thank you, no,” _____ said.

“Perhaps at a later date,” __ _____ added. “Right now our main interest is with Chagall. I’m sure you would agree that his color work is nonpareil.”

“What?” Jane asked. She stopped and turned to look at them, as though seeing them would help her understand.

They bent towards each other, conferring. _____ spoke first. “You perhaps do not have this equivalent word in your language. Peerless? Without rival?”

Jane relaxed. “Oh. Yes.” Her fingers brushed the headset, but it was just a word glitch. It happened occasionally. “Let’s continue.”

The Chagalls were not on exhibit, but rather set aside for the express purpose of today’s examination. Jane slid her keycard through the slot and opened the secure door that led to the storage vault where they had been prepared for viewing. The paintings were displayed on easels in the middle of the room, and a table held magnifying glasses for closer inspection.

Jane held out her hand. “We are pleased to be in possession of three original Chagalls—the first, on the left, is *Over Vitebsk*. That is dated at 1915-1920. The middle canvas is a nice contrast, called *The Firebird*, circa 1945. The last, to the far right there, is of course *I and the Village*, dated 1911.”

They moved to observe the canvases. Jane selected a magnifying glass from the table, but with no discernible optical organs, it suddenly seemed foolish—or worse—to offer Them a tool that relied on eyesight for use. She slid the lens into her pocket and watched Them.

They paused in front of each painting, but Jane could not decipher any speech. It had been noted that Their native communication relied on a frequency beyond human perception, so it was possible that They were speaking outside a range that she was able to detect, but the Kiev Convention had mandated that in mixed company both parties would agree to communicate in terms that everyone could understand. They seemed to be in compliance with the treaty thus far, so she doubted that They were in violation of the Convention. After a moment, __ _____ turned towards her and asked a question. "If I may be so bold to inquire, which is your personal favorite?"

Jane blinked. "I…I don't really like any of them, to be honest."

"Why?" _____ asked.

Jane looked at her hands. She couldn't believe she'd admitted that. "I mean, of course I enjoy art. It's why I went into this profession."

"Which artist do you prefer?" _____ asked.

Jane swallowed. "I guess I always liked Wyeth. Are you familiar with his work? We have *Ring Road* on exhibit in the North Gallery. It exemplifies his use of earth tones."

There was a moment of silence. Then, "The American. The Realist."

"Yes, but more than that," Jane said. "He showed a certain sensitivity. He was able to capture fragility in ordinary details. There is a magic in everyday life that he understood. He didn't need to resort to tricks to captivate. He saw the souls in people and in the land around him, and he showcased that on the canvas with just paint. Paint! It's the work of breathtaking genius. Truly humbling to behold."

"Tricks," _____ repeated. It wasn't a question. "Magic."

Jane frowned. "Not that I don't see worth in Chagall. It is just not a…personal favorite."

"*Mais lorsque nous capturons le vol d'une alouette en hiver, ne voyons-nous pas—*" Jane realized that she had hit the button that toggled between languages and she switched back just to hear the ending. "Yourself in it, just there?" __ _____ asked.

"I hope I did not offend you," Jane said, scrambling to cover the fact that she'd missed most of the sentence.

"Offend?" _____ asked. "Exchange of ideas is never offensive, little lark."

Jane touched her headset, wondering if she had a model that was prone to malfunction, or if she had missed something crucial in the exchange. She regretted, not for the first time, that she had not learnt another language in college when she had the chance. Now she merely nodded, although she wasn't sure quite why.

"We find the Chagall display satisfactory," __ _____ said after a long moment. "Thank you; you have been most helpful. We shall contact your agency if the need arises for re-examination."

"Wait," Jane said. "You barely looked at them! Are you sure you don't need anything else?"

_____ paused. "Our conversation has been most enlightening. We have found what we sought. You have our gratitude, Dr. Hysell. We shall now depart in peace."

Jane watched Them sway and flutter, then before she could articulate her formal valediction she found herself alone in the room with only three Chagalls for company.

The Creature from the Lake

Casey Ellis

1.

"If you'd never seen it before, this would look beautiful."

Margo had that same thought every morning when she went to dump synthetic meat in the lake. Despite the lake's undeniable beauty, she never managed to feel any better.

"It really is just the heat, sweetheart," her father always insisted. "If we lived in one of the cold areas a few miles east you wouldn't feel so bad. Oh, cold is no fun, but you want to do things, you know? You want to do things to avoid it. Heat you just can't avoid. You know?"

Margo sneered as always. As far as her father was concerned, she would never know what he wanted to say. But secretly, she knew. If it would ever change, if just once it felt cool, but instead it rained. Always warm though. A lot like urine. Sometimes, when the sky was grey, Margo would pretend that such a thing as autumn still existed and that it had arrived to take revenge on the warmth that had smothered it for so long. Other days, she would dream of running away to one of the cold areas.

Then she would instantly attack herself. The idea of leaving the lake was insane. They were lucky to have it. It had been Sarcodaemon-free for less than two years. Her father was not an arrogant man, but one thing he had a swellhead over was getting them out of the camps. It *had* been a miracle, getting this kind of assignment. What had been done for it?

"Lord almighty, is that really something to ask? We're out, you know? There's nothing more to say about it. Some things, you can't hold it against a person for doing everything to get out of, you know? Remember the camps? You were young, but I bet you remember."

Margo did. She also knew, whatever her father did, she herself would have done far worse to get out of there. Most of all, she remembered the guards, not with a curse like her father, but for a particular moment. One of the many riots that broke out stuck in her mind. The guards had to beat the crowd back with clubs. Regular guards didn't get guns. The human race couldn't afford too many losses. Usually, her father kept her pretty far away from such things. For one reason or another, he failed this time. She had not been hurt which was surprising, but she had seen something. Tears. Tears everywhere and from everyone. The people rioting had tears in their eyes. So did the guards, even the most sadistic. So did the man who shoved Margo into the mud to get away from someone else. Margo cried too.

She noticed it more after that. Everyone in the camps was always crying in some way, to some degree. During the almost daily rapes, Margo was only mildly surprised to notice that the rapists sometimes cried more than the victims. It was the same with the people who beat, stomped on and spat at people for no obvious reasons. Victims of these actions in the camps tended to be dead inside. Their tears were instinctive. If you had any fight left, you hurt other people. Over and over again. But it didn't help. Of course, there were a few left who only defended themselves and maybe one other person. Like Margo's father. Even these people did pretty ugly things to survive and save their loved ones. Love and survival were possible in the camps but heroism was simply out of the question.

No. It was better to be here. Here you only picked at yourself slowly. Margo would hate her father. Then she would remember the camps and hate herself. Either way, at least these emotions moved somewhat. Some things, most things, didn't change even to just change back again.

For example, regardless of the hatred concealed within her, every day she still had to throw the meat into the lake. She did it slowly this morning, carefully tossing the various chunks into the shallow end, always making sure never to cross the red painted line in the sand made by whoever had managed the lake area before her father. The tentacles came up out of the sand in the shallow end and grabbed the meat, pulling it back under the wet, shifting silt. Once in a while, Margo would throw a piece of the meat onto the dry part of the beach. A tentacle, long and light-pink, would snap right up and grab the food. What this thing was… that was anyone's guess.

It wasn't just the old creatures that had come back or the regular ones that had gone nuts. New ones, horrible ones were everywhere, and Sarcodaemons were hardly the worst. Few could be studied. Margo and her father had been warned that if they crossed the painted line, they would be pulled under. The tentacles could come further out, but for whatever reason, they wouldn't if they were fed every morning. That was the main function of Margo and her father: feeding the tentacles. Her father made up all sorts of other tasks for them, but it never helped Margo feel like anything other than a piece of the scenery. She had this one minor function, and otherwise, she was just background. That's probably what most of the stations around the world were like. The keepers were just background. Maybe that was the point of this whole thing.

2.

"Margo. A star, a great star, a true star. She never will be anything else or anything less."

"God."

"Have I ever told you about that movie? You're named for someone in it, you know?"

"GOD YES!" She had been planning to yell for days. This climax was not the welcome release she expected.

"Honey, I just, I just…you know."

Between anger and guilt, there wasn't much Margo could spit out. She stalked out of the little hut and onto the beach. If only there weren't so many trees, she *would* make a run for it. Sure she'd be killed, but at least she would die running. No way, though. The jungle was so thick she'd get killed tangled in some branches. That would be so pathetic even death wouldn't rid her of the humiliation.

Suddenly, Margo felt arms grabbing her from behind. Her father never touched her. She screamed and whirled around. Her father backed off.

"Oh god! I'm sorry baby! I just—you know—I just thought…I thought you were going to pass the line. I thought you were going to kill yourself. Not that I could blame you, but I'd…"

Her father started to weep softly. That broke it. Margo embraced him.

"I'm sorry, Daddy. I don't know why I hurt you. It isn't that I want to."

"You're not to blame. You aren't meant for this. I don't think anybody is. Kids, young people, they used to run out and play. You know, in the streets, out there."

"I know you're telling the truth, but I just can't believe that."

"Can't blame you, you know. I wish you could feel special. I wish I could. I gave you that name because it was special. Not like me. Bill. Pfff! Not much of a name. But I wanted there to be something you could say was special about you. Your mother hated it. 'Why name her after a character in a movie that's lost forever?' It was a special movie to me though, you know. I'm sorry, rambling…"

"Don't worry, Daddy."

"Just wish we could feel special. All people used to feel special once in a while. Now, we're just…scenery. You know?"

"I know, Daddy. I really do. Can you give me a few minutes? Then you should tell me that movie's story. It's been too long."

"Ok! Sure, I'll see you in a little bit."

3.

Margo sat on the beach, her head in her hands. The idea of feeling special. She could imagine it only as someone can imagine a place they've never even seen a photograph of. It was beautiful, breathtaking but so unreal, so far away.

She looked up, ready to go inside when she saw something new. It was lying just a few inches from the water. It looked like a fish at first, but…that head! Margo's instinct was to go get it, but despite all the pain she'd been through, she still wanted to live. The urge to go and pick up the creature was, however, almost overpowering.

"What is it?" she whispered to herself.

One of the tentacles came up out of the lake. This was the first time Margo had ever seen one of them emerge when it wasn't feeding time. The tentacle hovered daintily in the air for a moment. Then, suddenly, it tapped the creature three times, pushing it almost to the painted line. Whatever the creature was, it certainly wasn't moving and it rolled like a rock. The tentacle returned to hovering in the air.

Margo had already made her decision. Better to die than to ignore this message. She crossed the line. The tentacle did nothing. She picked up the creature which was cool and smooth but not slimy in the least bit. Still nothing. She walked back over the line. The tentacle withdrew back under the wet sand in the shallow end of the lake.

Back inside, her father was perplexed but philosophical. They both looked at the creature several times, unable to take their eyes off it for very long. Margo would have sworn it was a statue if she hadn't felt the obviously fleshy surface with her own hands. The bottom half was like any fish, with a tail fin, scales and all. The top half though, looked like the head, neck and chest of a young man. No doubt about it, an ordinary young man. The color of the whole creature was a very dark shade of green and there was no hair on the head, but otherwise, the top half looked totally human.

The expression was what kept them both entranced. It was a sad look but with no pain. Resigned and serene, the creature stared through tearless eyes at them both, feeling and understanding everything.

"Are you going to report it?" Margo finally asked quietly.

Her father thought for a much longer time than was usual for him before finally speaking.

"No, honey. This one I don't think we'll mention to anybody. Some things are just too special to be tagged and catalogued. This creature, the lake wanted us to see it, you know? But I don't think we should keep it."

They brought the creature back to the beach. Margo's father walked past the line without hesitation. Nothing happened. He walked right up to the lake and carefully placed the creature in the water. Still nothing. He and Margo were about to return home when they heard the voice. Thin, low and sexless, it seemed to come first from the lake. Then, it seemed to come from everywhere.

"Now…now…now…now…now…you see? You see. You know? You know."

Margo and her father stood, unable to move, listening, consumed by the first wonder either had felt in a long time.

"Then…then…then…then…then…peace. Peace. Peace. Peace."

A sudden chill cut through the air. Somewhere, in the back of his mind, Bill remembered that it was November.

The Dust Gets Into Everything

Jack Bates

Two years after a billionaire laid the foundation for putting humans on Mars, the race to colonize the red planet was on. The first group Jonathon Grantham sent consisted of two men, two women, and three humanoid looking robots they affectionately called Jerry, George, and Cosmo. Collectively the robots were known as Hipster Doofuses. The human crew had a more professional moniker: the Pioneers. Their privately funded transport had been christened the Mayflower II by their sponsor.

Jerry, George, and Cosmo spent a month securing the modular structures the billionaire had sent a year before he sent the humans. There were five rectangular boxes similar in size to shipping containers stacked high on freighters. One served as a bunkhouse, another as a kitchen and dining area where they would grow their own vegetables. The third served as a gym-slash-entertainment center with two working toilets and showers while the fourth was a working laboratory. The final pod was the mechanical heart of the small settlement; it also housed the Doofuses.

The Doofuses attached pressurized walkways between the five modules. The four humans guided the robots and monitored the progress from inside the Mayflower II. Each morning the Doofuses exited one of the modules through a pressurized door on the side of a module. Each night they returned the same way. The human crew waited patiently in the MFII. Once they were moved in to Mars Base Virginia, the Mayflower II would be converted into an emergency escape vehicle in the event of a highly unlikely emergency.

Everything went as planned. Back on Earth, Jonathon Grantham was heralded. He hosted lavish parties. Heads of State celebrated his accomplishment and secretly negotiated with him to start carving up the landscape for their governments.

While all of this was going on, the four humans living on the red planet increasingly became concerned over what at first appeared to be an insignificant irritation. In their transmission back to the command center in Arizona, they didn't initially mention it. One of the crew, a woman named Kinsler, who served as Chief Medical Officer, first voiced her concern at dinner after repeated attempts to rectify the situation failed.

"Have you noticed," she asked breaking off the corner of a nutrition wafer "the dust?"

Yuri Krozek, a Russian biologist, shook his head. "It's nothing, Residual from when the Doofuses were connecting the walkways. We clean soon."

"I feel like we've been cleaning since we got here," Kinsler said.

Kinsler ran her finger over the table. A fine dusting of a puce colored powder covered her finger tip. She held it out for Krozek and Walt Henderson, the pilot, to see. She rubbed her thumb over it. Instead of smearing it away the dust seemed to increase in size. She sniffed her finger tips. "Smells like cooked meat."

Sheila Abbott, the other female of the Pioneers, carried over a bowl full of salad. "Well there was nothing in the vegetables that didn't wash off. And we don't know for certain it's Martian soil. Who knows where Grantham got these units or how long they sat where they did. I mean, cooked meat? Maybe these things once housed slabs of beef."

Kinsler wasn't buying it. "These crates sat up here for nearly a year before we got here. It was another couple of weeks before Jerry, George, and Cosmo got them connected. That was a lot of down time for the dust to build up."

"Right. Residual." Krozek said. "We clean up after dinner."

The others began heaping salad on their plates. Kinsler lifted hers and blew on it. A small cloud puffed up off of the surface. She set her plate back on the table and chewed on her nutrient wafer.

"You have to eat," Abbott said. "You can't let the little things get to you. There's nowhere to go. You're a member of this mission after extensive psychological and physical testing."

Kinsler's face felt warm. Her three comrades watched her. Abbott, of course, was right. Back on Earth who knew how much junk got into her food, how many bugs she had eaten. What harm could there be in a little dust? Besides, wasn't dust mostly shed human skin?

Still, it wasn't that easy to shake the uncertainty that came with living on Mars. Kinsler knew it would be at least two years before she could even consider the three month return trip to home.

Two years unless they used the emergency pods the Doofuses worked on almost daily when Abbott wasn't sending them for soil and rock samples.

Kinsler wiped her plate before she took a small pinch of the salad. Abbott slid her a small packet of Italian dressing. Kinsler opened one, squeezed it onto her meal, and took a bite. The lettuce was a little soft, as was the freeze dried tomato. The onion strips crunched nicely. The peppers tasted a little stale. But even as she finished chewing she could feel the grit on her tongue, between her teeth. None of her team showed any indication of experiencing the same. They talked and laughed and ate while Kinsler ate less and less of her meal. Even the tofu cubes felt powdery.

Afterwards, while Krozek performed maintenance on the indoor garden and Abbott checked the day's data as gathered by the Doofuses who were now in their housing bays for Henderson to clean, Kinsler gave the kitchen pod a thorough cleaning. Twice. She ran the same finger over the same spot on the table, then on the stainless steel prep counter, even over the floor. For the first time in days she felt she was free of the dust.

Henderson's voice came over the intercom. "Kinsler. Can you come to the mechanical module?"

She pressed the Talk button. "Be right there."

Krozek looked up from his pruning. He gave her a curious smile. Kinsler shook her head. She passed through the bunkhouse and then the entertainment center where Abbott looked up from her computer. She offered Kinsler a look that would have mirrored Krozek's if they had been in the same room.

"I thought he was checking on how the dust is getting in here," Kinsler said.

Abbott tipped her head to the side. "He's been in the mechanical room since after dinner. You know, Chris, we're living on a desert planet. There's going to be dust."

"Not like this. It's growing."

"We have twenty-two months before we're relieved. We have to get this place ready for the first wave of colonists. Grantham will be sending the next modules and crews in a few months."

"I realize that, June. What are you getting at?"

"It's just dust. Vacuum it up."

Kinsler proceeded into the last pod. She found Henderson kneeling in front of George adjusting what would be the knee joint on a human. Henderson coughed a couple of times before he realized she was there.

"Hey. I think I found where your dust is coming from." He stood up but not without supporting himself with a hand on George's chest. He coughed into the elbow pit of his opposite arm. It was a dry sounding cough.

"You okay, Henderson?" Kinsler asked.

"Throat's a little scratchy."

"I'm going to start you on antibiotics," Kinsler said. "Last thing we need up here is some kind of flu bug."

"Yeah, yeah. Okay. But the dust. I think it's coming in with the Doofuses." He coughed several more times. He shook his head. "Excuse me. Woo. I've gotten enough dust off of them to fill a five gallon jug. It's put George on the disabled list. Just when I think I've cleaned it all out I find more. I'm going to take it into the lab and—" Henderson fell into a coughing fit.

"Not right now you aren't. You're going to your bunk. Abbott can run the analysis."

Henderson nodded. He coughed a few more times. Kinsler led him into the lab where she injected a super antibiotic into his arm. He coughed often enough that Abbott looked up from the computer.

"Is he all right?" she asked after Henderson left.

Kinsler stared down the short, empty, walkway. "I don't know."

None of them heard Henderson die during the night. He went peacefully. Krozek brought in Jerry and Cosmo to move Henderson into a body bag. George was no longer operational. When the two remaining Doofuses lifted Henderson, his limbs pulled free. Sand poured from what now looked like a dried out old husk.

Abbott screamed. Eventually, Kinsler had to sedate her.

Krozek took up the task of cleaning up the dust that had been Henderson. He separated a small amount for Kinsler to analyze in the lab. She could hear the heavy duty shop vacuum, slightly unnerved at the disposal of her crewmate.

Kinsler ran the tests twice, looked at the results, and ran it a third time. Each test offered the same results. There was a typical amount of silicates and metals in the dust associated with the surface of Mars. The individual grains averaged about twenty-five micrometers in diameter. As far as Kinsler could tell, there was nothing in the dust to indicate Henderson had ever existed.

She pushed her chair closer to the wall. Her thumb pressed down on the Talk button of the intercom. "Yuri, can you come to the lab?"

She lifted her thumb. There was a fine coat of dust on her skin. She rubbed it together with her finger then proceeded to slide her fingers back and forth over her palm. Within moments she had a small pile of gritty dust in her hand. She dumped it into a Petri dish then rubbed her palms together to clean her hands.

A fine shower of dust fell into her lap.

Kinsler covered her hands with an antibacterial solution. It was the only thing that took away the gritty feeling. She used her elbow to press the Talk button a second time to call Krozek. When she didn't get an answer, she hurried through the walkways to the dining pod.

Krozek looked like he was in the Child's Pose for a yoga class. His arms were pulled in at his sides. His knees were tucked under his belly. His forehead touched the floor. It looked as if he were praying to the sandbox that had once been the garden.

Kinsler knew he was dead. She didn't want to touch him, but she had to be certain. Gingerly, she lifted his head off the ground. Dust poured from his open mouth, his nostrils. Each of his eyes burst and dust poured from his sockets. As the grit flowed, his head deflated. The remaining dust filled his belly until that ruptured. Dust flowed out over Kinsler's slippers.

She screamed. Her feet would never feel clean, even if she somehow managed to get home.

Kinsler knew then she would never have that opportunity. Home was millions of miles and endless days through space away. Before long, the next craft of colonists would be on their way. She had to prevent them from leaving Earth. Grantham would just have to take the loss.

Above her a red light flashed. The breach alarm sounded. The dining compartment was about to lose integrity.

Kinsler hurried through the walkway. She sealed the passage at both ends. She went to the bunkhouse and did the same. Abbott slept peacefully. Kinsler knew she had to wake her. There was no way she could get her inside the pressure suit on her own. Then she wondered what difference it would make? The dust got into everything, didn't it? It had no problem getting into their climate controlled and sealed fortress.

Yet that basic instinct of survival pushed Kinsler to not surrender.

She gave Abbott a shot of adrenaline. Abbott sat up.

"Are those the alarms?" Abbott asked.

"I don't have time to explain," Kinsler said. "Krozek is dead. We have to get into the pressure suits."

"And then what?"

"We go to the emergency pod. The solar panels have had plenty of time to build up power to shoot us out of here."

"I can't get in one of those."

"Then stay here and die."

"It's like being in a coffin."

"You'll be asleep until a rescue crew is sent for us."

"I can't do it, Chris."

"Fine. But I'm not dying here."

"Wait. Where are you going?"

"Grantham and the base have to be warned it's not safe here."

"Why now? Why us?"

Kinsler stopped. "What do you mean?"

"I mean all those probes, all those years they sat here sending us pictures or drilling stone or collecting samples. They survived. Hell, a few of them are still sending us feeds from the far side of the planet. Those machines are fine. Why aren't we?"

Kinsler stared at Abbott. She shook her head. "I don't know. But Earth has to be told to stay away."

"Chris?"

"What is it, June?"

"I'm coming with you."

"Get in your pressure suit. I'll be right there."

Kinsler went into the lab. She sent a mayday over the telescreen. She had to use a minivac to clean away the control panel before she could use it.

"This is Mars Mission One Chief Medical Officer Christine Kinsler. Listen carefully. Abort all future missions to Mars. It's the dust. I can't explain it but it's everywhere and in everything. Science Officer Yuri Krozek and Chief Pilot Walter Henderson are both dead because of it."

Kinsler paused. She searched for a way to say it and finally just told it like it was.

"I know this sounds insane. I am not experiencing any type of psychosis. Each man died filled with dust and then crumpled away. The same thing happened to the plants in the garden. Structural integrity is fading as the pods rust away around us. Science Officer June Abbott and I are preparing the escape pods. Send help immediately to our distress signal."

Kinsler paused again. She stared at the camera bubble on the consul in front of her. A fine coating of dust was covering the lens. She wiped it with her sleeve then showed it to the camera.

"See? It's everywhere. It coats everything. It gets in everywhere. Henderson thought it was coming in with the bots. It might have started that way but it grows. It expands. Think of an oil spill and how it just keeps getting bigger and bigger. Look, just stay away. I am leaving now."

She went back to the bunkhouse to put on her pressure suit and to see what was taking Abbott so long. Inside the module she found Abbott standing in the center of the room wearing her suit. Her helmet was on with the radiation shield engaged over her face.

Kinsler took her own pressure suit from the cupboard.

"Sorry I took longer than I thought I would. It just sounded so crazy as I was saying it." Kinsler secured the suit. She reached back into the cupboard for her helmet. "Grantham will think I've gone nuts, I'm sure. But you know I'm not, right, June?"

But June did not move.

"June?"

Kinsler stepped over to her friend. She took June's right arm in her hand. She felt the shift of sand beneath the sleeve. A second later the fingers of the glove broke open. Dust poured from the tips. Kinsler released her grip on the arm. It dropped to the side of Abbott's pressure suit. Kinsler reached out and lifted the radiation shield.

The glass facing of the helmet cracked. Sand rushed forward from the opening. Kinsler screamed. She shoved Abbott in the chest with both of her hands. Instead of toppling backwards the suit crumpled to the floor in a pile of dust.

Kinsler put on her helmet. She moved through the modules as walls ripped open like the thin skin of an overripe plum. In the last pod she found the Doofuses in their docking bays. Jerry and Kramer stood on either side of their incapacitated friend George. She felt a momentary twinge of guilt at leaving them behind until she realized they were just bots. They weren't sentient yet. It had been she and her crew that named them and treated them like clowns.

Maybe if Grantham had invested in artificial intelligence, her mission team would still be alive.

The escape pods were in an airtight bubble outside of the last module. They formed a ring of green ovals, each equipped with a bed and intravenous food supply that would be fed to the occupant. Kinsler punched in the code and a door hissed opened. She entered an antechamber. The door hissed closed behind her. Fans and vacuums quickly cleared the chamber of foreign substances. A green light flashed. Kinsler removed her pressure suit. She once more ran the vacuum and fans until she felt clean. Another code allowed her access to the pods. All four opened. She settled into one.

Once in, she had moments to activate the life support system. Her arms slipped into sleeves that would monitor her vitals and feed her. The computer counted down to lift off. It was the longest fifteen seconds of her life.

Just before the pod ring lifted off, two things happened.

Kinsler sneezed. She was only barely aware of the spot of dust she'd expelled onto the observation window because that was when the second event occurred.

Kinsler fell asleep. The sandman arrived. He gave her a lovely dream of open fields full of green grass and fragrant flowers under blue skies and a yellow sun. She dreamed this dream until night filled her head and the world grew cold.

It was a month later when the rescue craft finally located the distress beacon. The pod was pulled aboard the rescue ship. They found no survivors but in one of the pods they did find several pounds of a puce colored dust.

Universal Assemblage

Nathan Mark Phillips

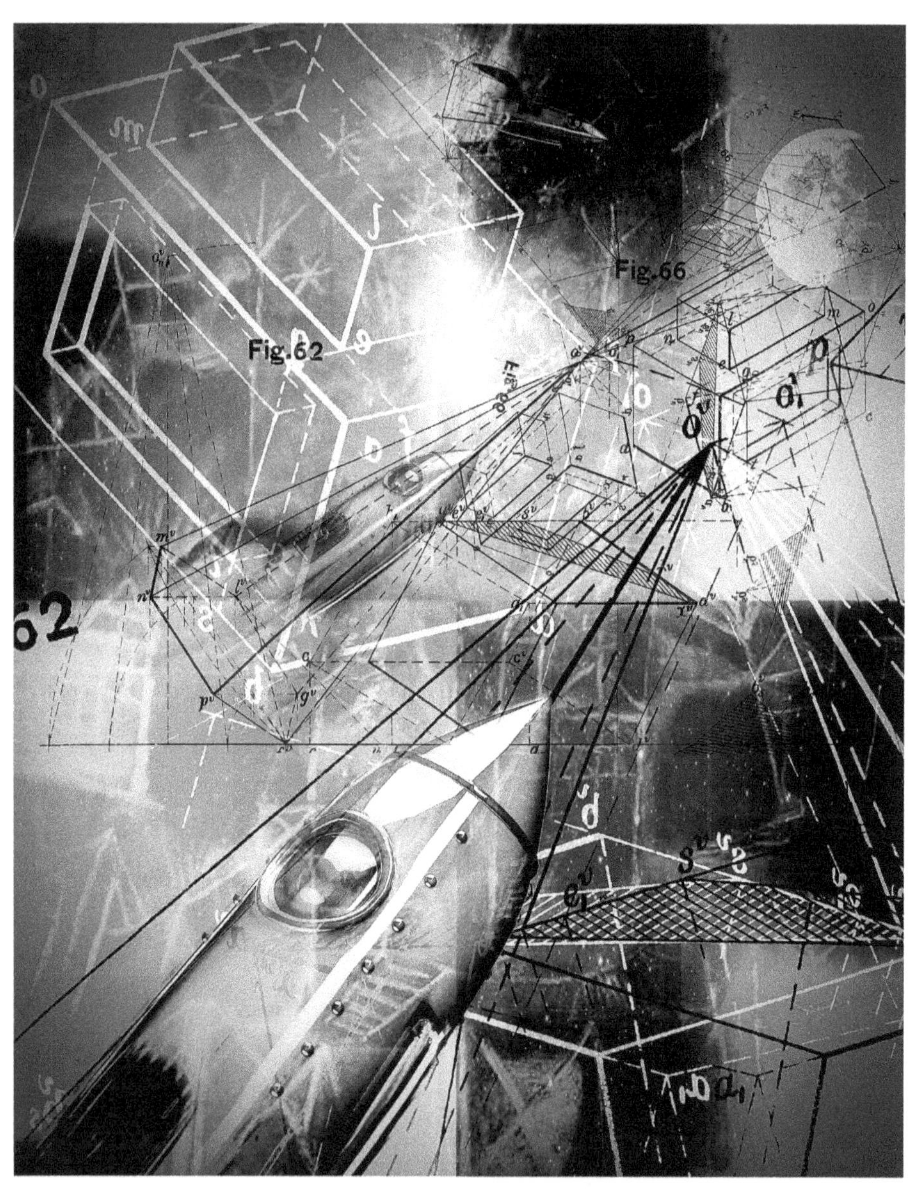
Fig.66
Fig.62
62

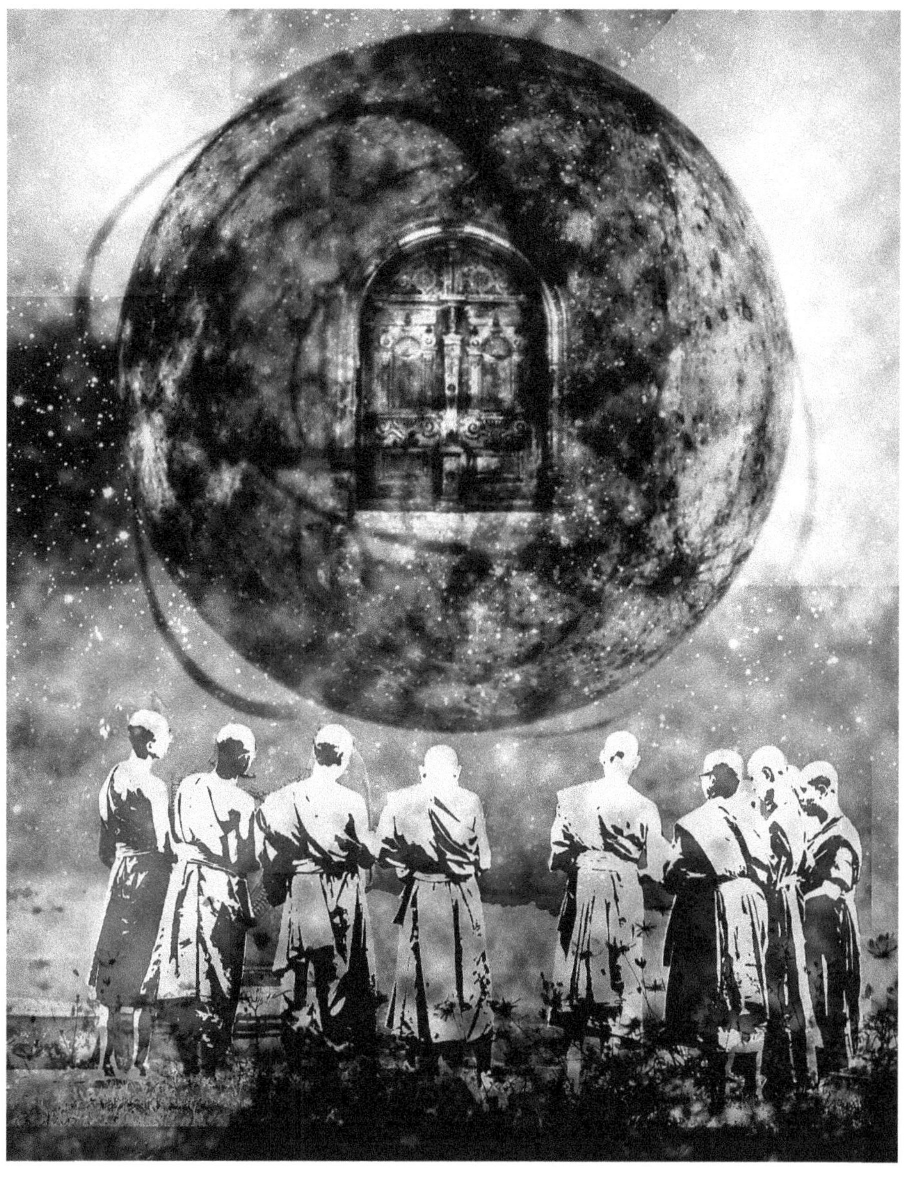

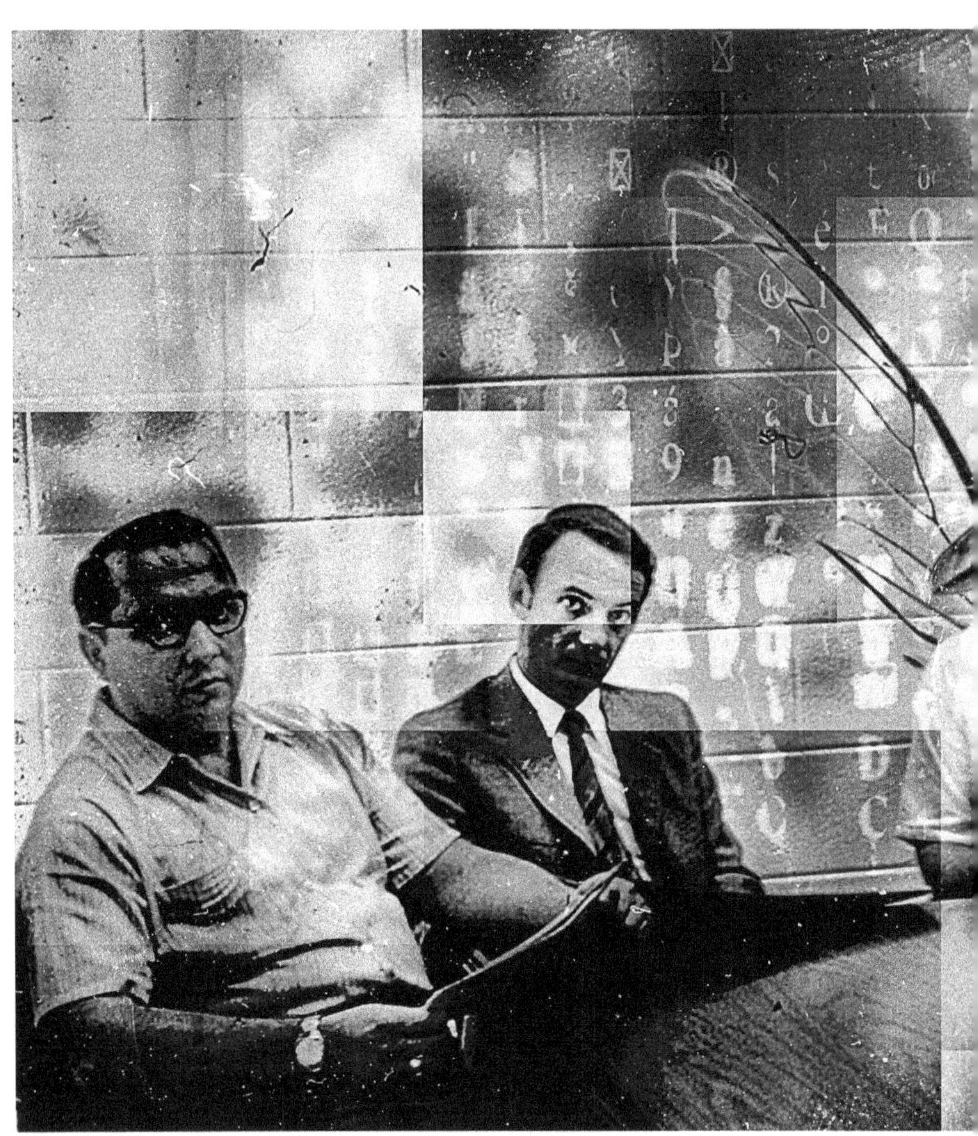

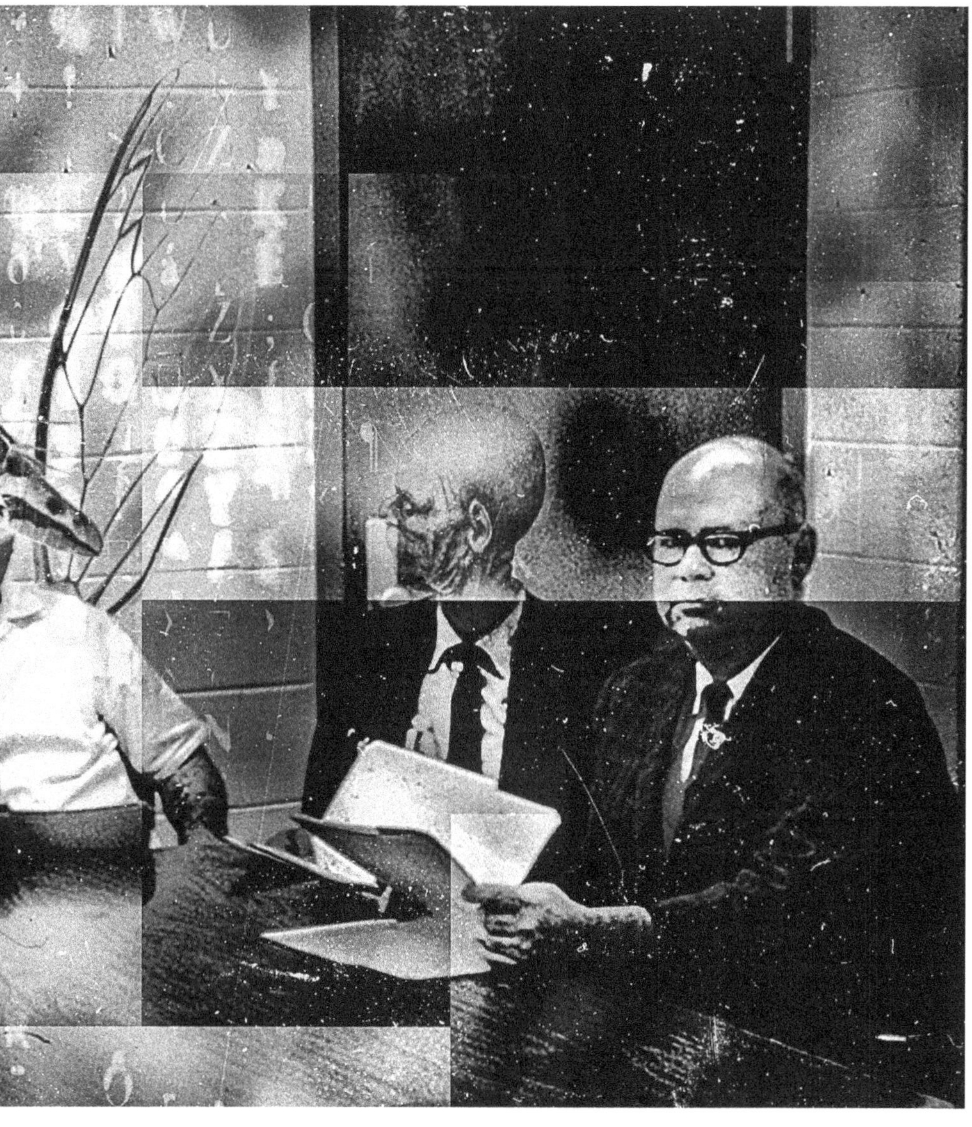

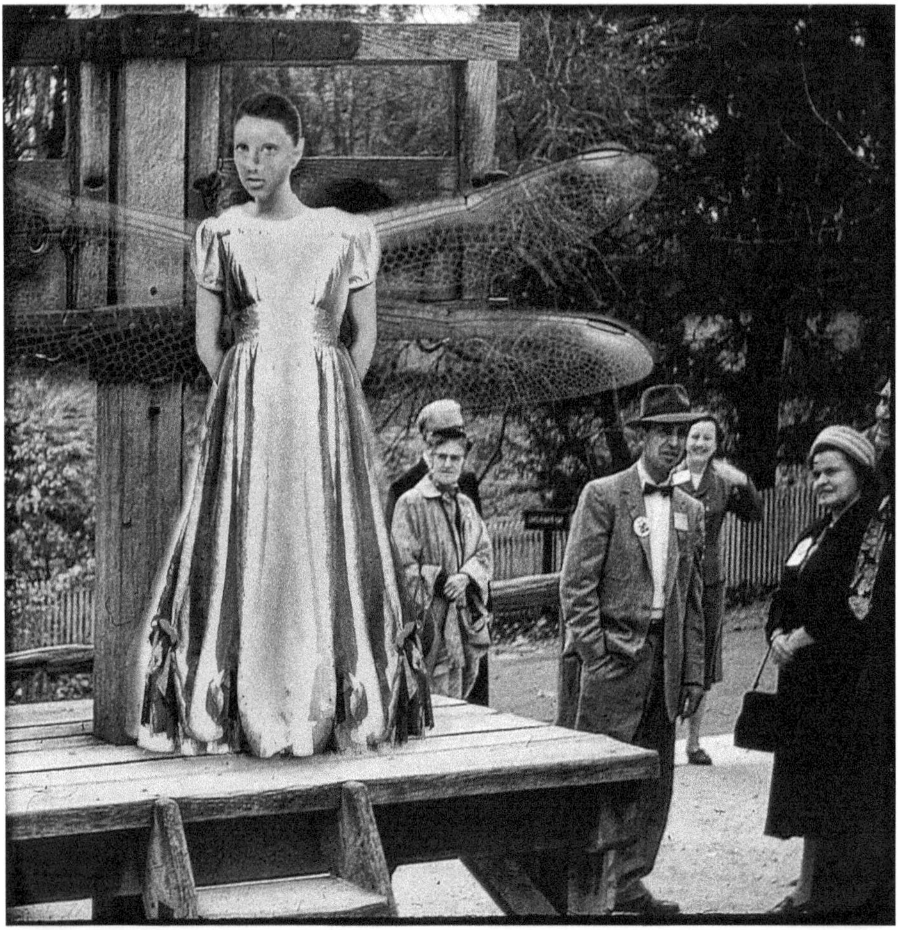

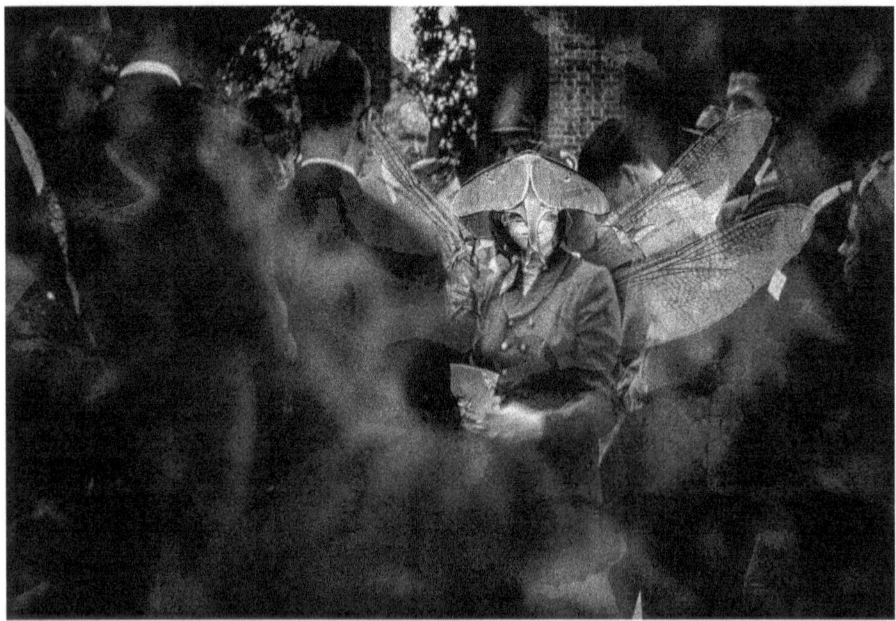

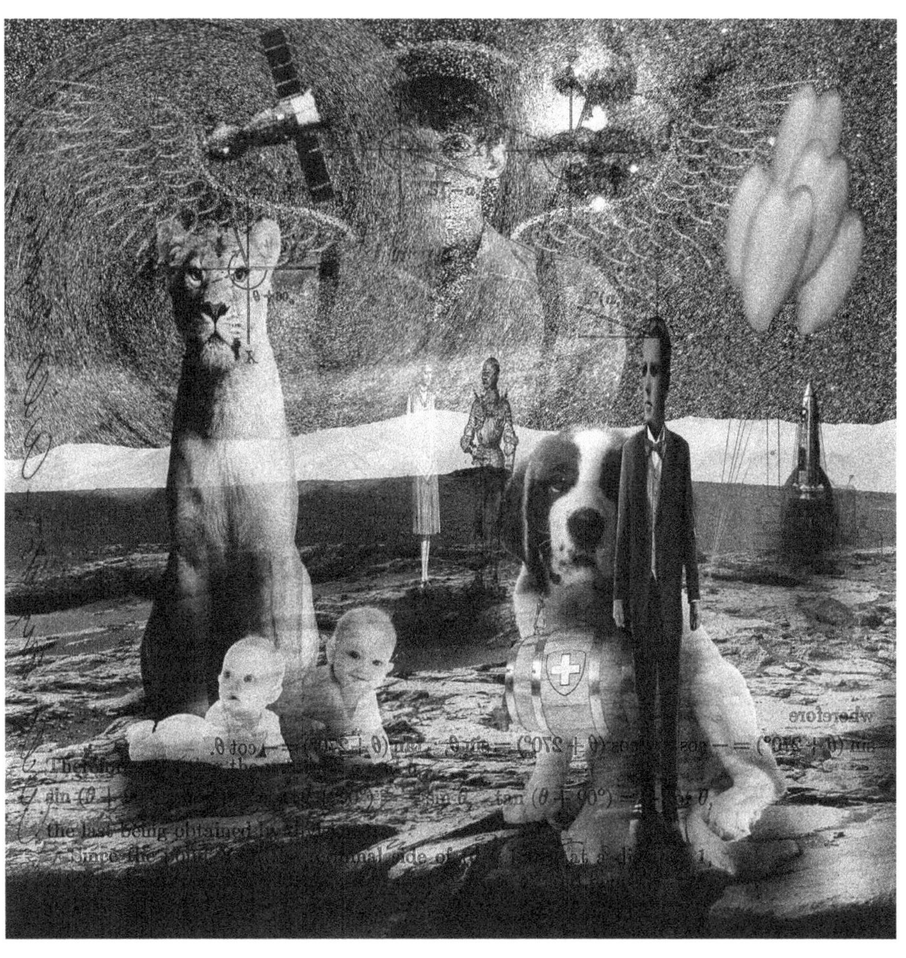

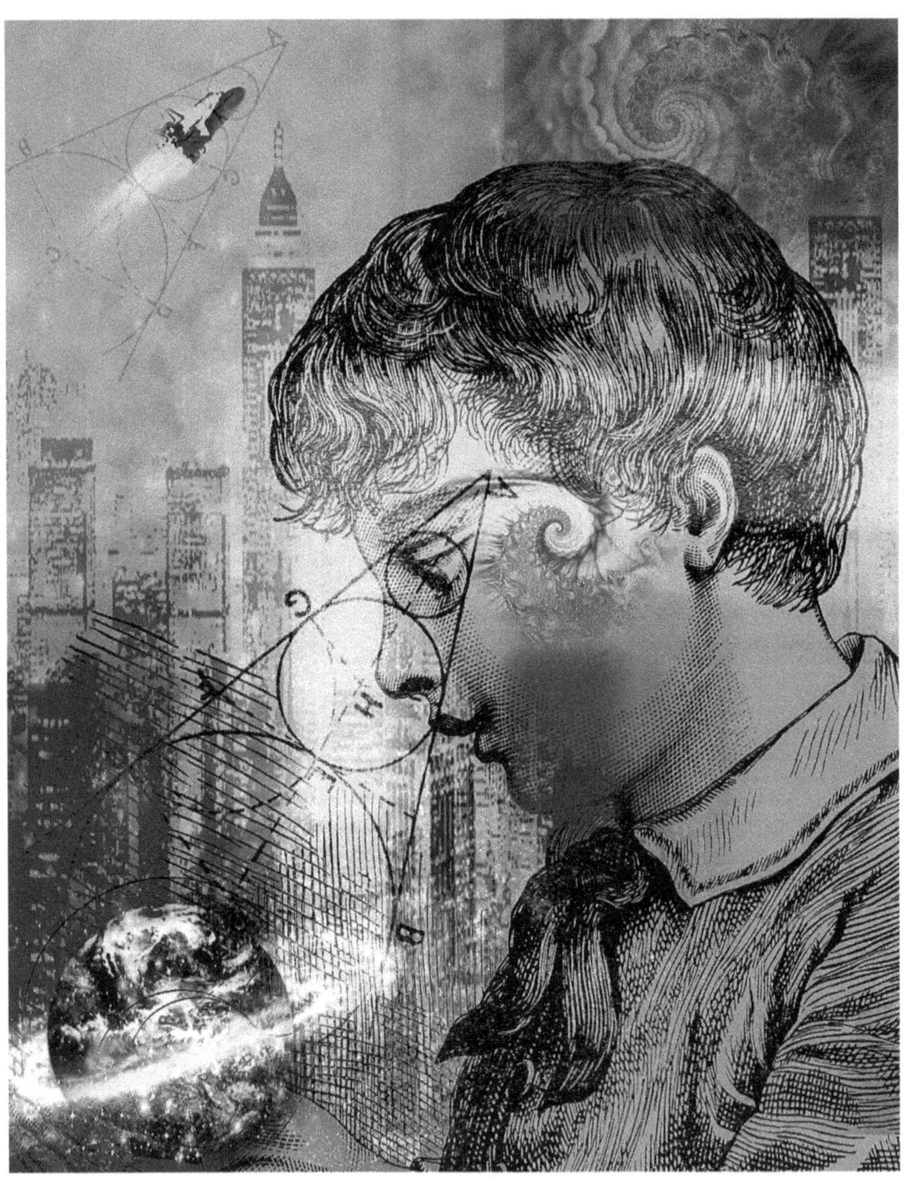

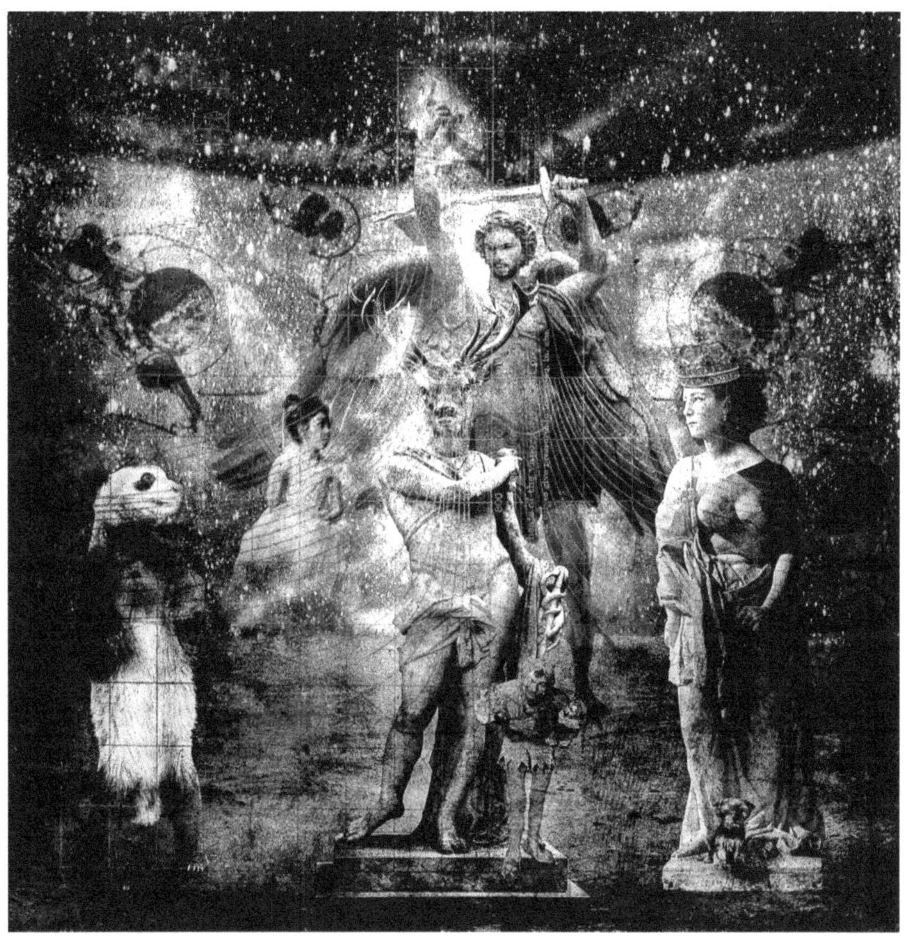

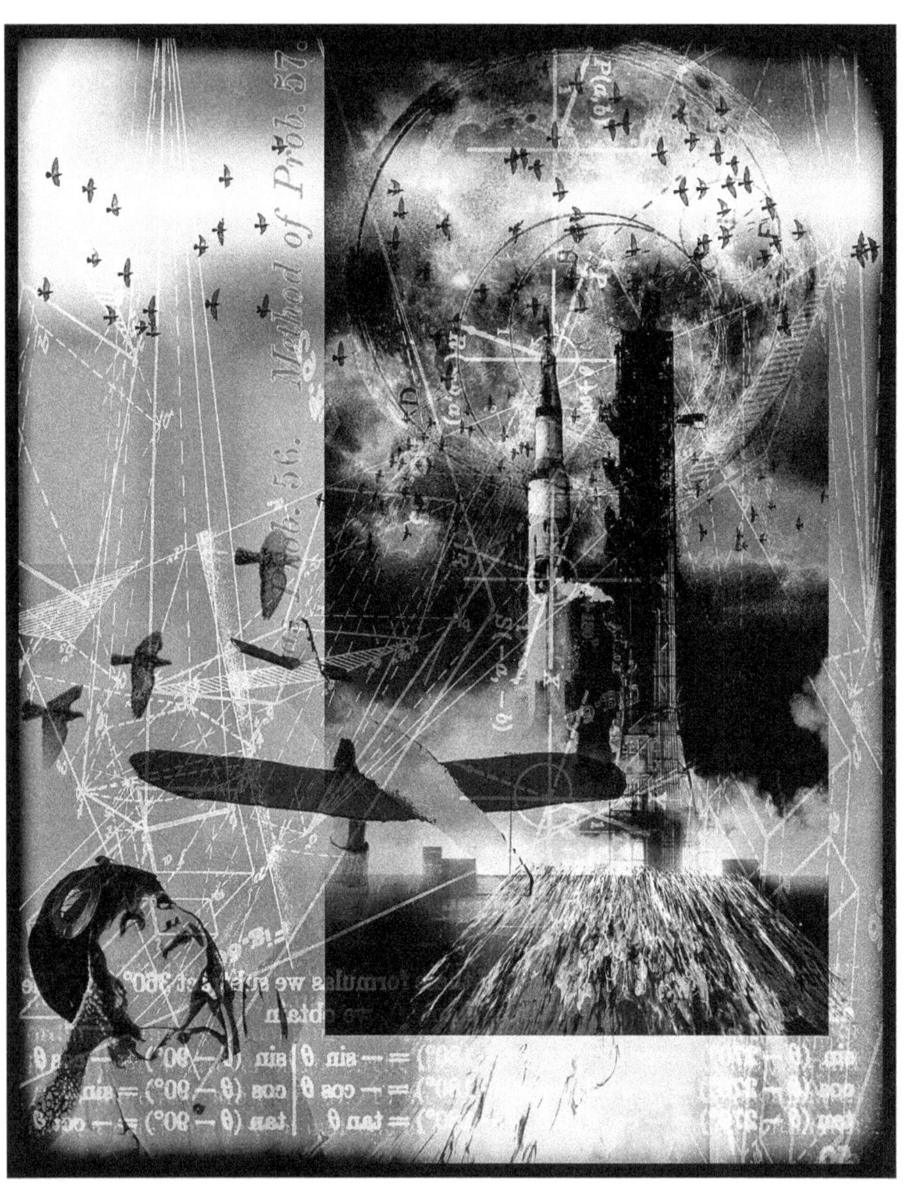
Prob. 56. Method of Prob. 57.

Fire Thirst

P.J. Schaefer

One day, the non-feeling became hatred or, at least, a burning, angry, explosive desire to hate—maybe just to feel something. I became consumed and, as once before I had built my life on the desire to love, then not to feel, I transformed, and instead knew only the obsession to avenge myself.

The plan was easy. I replayed it repeatedly in my mind. The two of them often went out together, leaving me alone. The two of them—the one who had never done anything with his son in those early years when the boy needed so much to be done for him and with him, and the one who had always been done for and spent hours and tears bemoaning the absence of his father and offering a thankfulness that I had always been there for him, chauffeured him everywhere, seen every game, advised on every homework assignment—now were inseparable. Now it was easy to be together, now that they had the common, unadmitted, guilt-ridden bond of avoidance of my haggard eyes. I planned to set my trap while they enjoyed some activity—fishing, golfing, kayaking, climbing—together and ignite it when they were alone and dosing unaware, never suspecting the calm, never-complaining me to strike.

The house, old and a ready-made firetrap, needed only a spark in the right place: the musty attic, filled with old sentimental junk I never should have saved anyway. The brown, dust-covered Seagram's Seven bottle lamp, a left-over from Bill's college days, our first apartment, and Patrick's first big boy room, needed but an adjustment of a wire and the wall socket. I saw it short and watched the little puff of smoke and knew the rest would smolder slowly, until eventually it caught. I placed it among the box of old poems and love letters I'd written Bill, buried it underneath the damp, curled pile. I turned the main light off and descended the stairs. I disconnected the smoke detectors on all three floors and in the basement.

I looked once into Patrick's bedroom, neat and tidy thanks to my handiwork, and snatched the little brown and ragged teddy bear from its suspended net in the far corner of the room. It had been his first teddy; Bill and I had shopped for it together, given it to him together, and, until he turned five years old and began making real friends, it had served as his "brother." I hugged it, stroked it but a moment, trying hard to remember those times of family, of energy, and could not. I stuffed the bear into my handbag and then cast my eyes into my own bedroom, resting, of all places, upon our wedding photo. I moved to it and ran my fingers around the frame, touched our faces, traced our outlines, trying to recognize the people there. *A dream,* I thought, *just a dream. But when did we lose it? Was it somewhere between our jobs, our relatives, our schedules, our growing so accustomed to one another that we took each other for granted, passing as known and forgotten entities like the stuffed bear? Was it tucked between the countless, routine actions which once expressed love, but accumulated until they became chores somewhere along the way? Was it lost among the unspoken needs and feelings of twenty-four years? Oh where is it now? What was it then?* I wondered.

I walked to the hallway, closed and locked the door, and moved to my car. As I opened the driver side door, the red AMC jeep pulled in, right on schedule, forty-five minutes late.

"Where are you going, Mom?"

"To run some errands. I'll be back in time to make supper." I leaned over and kissed Patrick on his way by and then kissed Bill as he passed.

An hour and a half later, I knew they lay on opposite ends of the couch in the basement recreation room, comfortably sleeping to some television show, magazines draped over their knees. I also knew the smoke would soon start filtering down to the second floor. I gazed out on the

Hudson again, the same water I had stared at for the last hour and ten minutes. I turned to face the park. A small child and her parents played together, laughing as they tackled each other. The little girl's thin, shaggy bangs hung in her eyes and as she pushed them back, she smiled at me.

I walked to the public phone. I called four fire stations and reported nonexistent fires, claiming my name and address from those I had read in the obituaries. They would all arrive too late at my house.

The little girl came giggling and running toward me, chasing her football. I bent, picked it up from its spot just in front of my feet and handed it to her. "Thank you," she blurted out, smiling at me for a second time. She returned to her parents, and as I watched them play, a single tear ran down my cheek.

I turned again to the phone. After twelve rings, Patrick answered groggily. "I need you and your father. I'm in Peekskill, at the waterfront. I've had an accident and I'll need both of you to get me and the car home. Are you coming? Patrick, did you get that?"

"Yeah, Ma." I hoped he'd be too sleepy to smell the smoke.

I climbed into my car. Twenty minutes later, the gravel of our driveway spat out under its tires. The jeep was gone. I could see the flames in the upstairs back window. I shut the car off, taking only my keys. I walked to the front door and unlocked it. The smoke had begun to fill the house, but I could still see the boys' clutter—the jackets, the boots, their paraphernalia, their snack bowls—strewn about the room. I picked it all up and put it in the closet. I walked toward the second floor. I could feel the heat as I stood on the landing. The flames danced, reached, stretched for something, something perhaps to feed them or to squelch them, and I reached for them, marched to them.

I never heard the sirens. I never felt or saw the man who dragged me out of the house. I remember nothing after joining the flames, those hot, out-of-control entities that swallowed me, and I them. Now, my skin is almost ready for the first graft. I cannot see. My teddy and I keep company. Patrick said I could keep him.

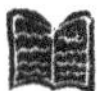

I'll Take Ashes

P.J. Schaefer

Margaret Mackevy settled into the beautician's chair without explanation. Dolores, the stylist, asked incredulously, "Shorter? If you go much shorter, you'll need a razor buzz-cut. Are you certain that's what you want? I remember when you had shoulder length hair not so long ago. You looked so different then."

"That's the whole point, isn't it?" Margaret almost said, but she nodded her assent instead. She stared silently and deliberately *away* from the mirror.

Dolores attempted to converse. "So, what's the occasion—

—wedding, baptism, big date?"

"Funeral," Margaret barely audibly replied, steeling herself for the inevitable condolences.

Dolores didn't recite the platitudes. "I don't think I'd cut my hair—or do anything with my hair or face or anything—for a funeral. It seems like a lot of trouble for a dead person, or else a lot of disrespect for him because you're fussing with yourself when you ought to be grieving for him."

Margaret turned slightly in her chair. "It's for my own funeral."

Dolores, always unflappable, remarked slowly, "Perhaps you'd like something really special then."

"No, that's the point; don't you see? Why look good at all? Why not look like the diminutive creature you are, consigned to nothingness, reduced to maggots or ashes?"

"I'd take ashes, myself. I wouldn't like to think about the fire, but the maggots and other critters in the ground would have to be worse. Blow dry today?"

Margaret nodded, and within minutes, she stood to leave the salon. As the door gradually closed behind her, she could just hear the remarks Dolores had begun to make to her co-workers. "Get that one! As if any of us knows when, exactly, we will die."

We do if we pay attention, Margaret thought. *I didn't pay attention soon enough.*

Margaret went next to the florist's shop two blocks south. She flipped through a display leaflet several times, peered into the refrigerated glass cabinet repeatedly, and paced. She could not decide. "What," she whispered to herself, "is the color of unfulfilled dreams, of mistaken perceptions, of loss?"

"May I help you?"

Margaret blinked twice. "Yes, I seek a very small funeral arrangement, something that can stand in a vase."

"Would you like a banner with that, 'For Loving Mother,' or something like that?"

"'Beloved child' would suffice."

"And when and where do you need the arrangement?"

"Sometime today, please, at this address." Margaret passed the florist a crumpled piece of paper.

The florist scrutinized the writing on the paper.

"But this is not the address of any funeral home I know. It's located in the residential section. It's a private home."

"Yes, I want to take the arrangement to the funeral myself. Is that a problem?"

"It's extremely unusual, but I suppose we can do it."

Margaret paid the woman and left the shop. She proceeded next to the pharmacy right near the funeral home where she had already chosen the urn she wanted. Phil, the head pharmacist smiled when he saw her. They had once worked together, when Margaret had needed part-time, paying, steady cashier work to support herself while she tried to get her freelancing career started and succeeding. "I'll bet I know what you need today. Hold on a minute, and I'll key up the script to see if it has any remaining renewals."

Margaret scanned the shelves while she waited. She checked the tobacco products aisle, where she found the lighter fluid she needed. She perused the magazine racks, staring maliciously at the glossy covers of vibrant young stars airbrushed to perfection, splashy titles etched across them in bold whites, blues, and blacks. Once, she thought these magazines had held substance, but now she believed they simply cloned glitz, scandal, and beauty tips. She selected instead one of the bestselling, paperback mysteries. She knew she would spend her evening reading it.

Morning dawned brightly, the sun streaming through the blinds Margaret never fully closed. She had hoped for rain—or at least an overcast sky—for this day. She shrugged, rose, showered, and donned the black dress she always used for funerals. She drank her tea slowly and then went to the secluded backyard of her home. She had prepared the funeral pyre the previous night, and it stood ready, awaiting only the lighter fluid and the flame of one match. Encased in a metal contraption she had fashioned from four now empty filing cabinets and their drawers, the pile stretched five feet high and almost as many feet across. Its bottom layer consisted of reference books—dictionaries, thesauruses, writing manuals—and sitting on top of those lay at least fifty bestsellers—the books of celebrities and their ghost writers as well as those penned by authors currently enjoying bestselling status. Largest of all loomed the stacks upon stacks of paper, thousands of pages, each of them filled with typed words, many of them scratched across and altered in pencil, some of them photocopied rejection letters. Teetering at the top of the carefully constructed mound rested exactly seventy-eight, three-hundred-page journals, each of them overflowing with words.

Margaret stepped over to the pile, gingerly crowning it with the prescription eye drops she would no longer need and the funereal floral arrangement she had purchased. She surveyed the pyre once more, needing its drama and ritual, its physical symbol as much as the flame would need oxygen to burn. Deliberately and slowly, she retrieved the lighter fluid and drenched the pile in it. At last, she was ready to ignite the pyre, to complete the very palpable, concrete act that would prove her freedom and signify her change and her decision. The match scratched loudly against the rough surface of the matchbox and hissed for a moment. Margaret touched it to the bottom of the pile and watched as little flames began to catch the paper. Gradually, the flames grew, stretching, reaching for the top and more oxygen, their yellow-orange-white-blue glow almost mesmerizing. As Margaret closed the lid of her homemade incinerator, watching the smoke curl and rise and the flames dance, she whispered to herself, "Old dreams squelched, new ones rising; old me dead, new me born." She listened to the crackling of the fire, staring hard at the progress of the flames, and for the first time in many months, she smiled. "I'll take ashes, too," she murmured to herself, thinking she would save the ashes in the urn as a reminder to herself the next time she considered chasing a dream and a passion.

Margaret did not quite see the tiny flame that inched its way out from underneath the incinerator, caught the grass, and began moving its way toward her, following the lighter fluid trail she had inadvertently left. The flames reached her feet before she even realized what had happened, and instinctively, she began stamping at them. She had reacted too slowly, though, and the flames began to climb up the barbecue grill, toward the propane gas tank. Quickly, Margaret turned to the back door, thinking she would get her fire extinguisher and squelch the blaze before it did too much damage. Already, her eyes burned with the smoke, and panic began to rise in her chest. She had to fiddle with the screen door handle for several, precious seconds before she managed to pull it open. Then she discovered she had locked herself out of the house. She pounded on the door in frustration, wishing the door had a window she could smash.

Margaret turned, surveying the flames that by then surrounded her. Her make-shift incinerator had not withstood the heat and fire and lay fallen and wilted, replaced by an uncontained bonfire. She searched for a hole through which she could escape, and just as she thought she had found one, the heat of the fire finally ignited the grill's gas, and the explosion startled her so much that she reacted by ducking, and then found herself on the ground, facing the flames at eye level. The flames leapt at her, as if exhibiting a life and desire of their own: the wish to consume her. She rose, patting down her clothing and blinded by smoke. She tried to peer over her yard's fence to discern if any neighbors were awake, but she could see no lights. She screamed for help anyway, and then made a desperate run out of the flames, only to find herself engulfed by them and running toward the pyre. She knew she had to reach the gate at the horizontal end of the yard to get to the front of the house and away from the conflagration.

Her dress caught fire first, and she immediately dropped to the ground to smother the flames' progress, but she fell upon burning grass. She could not think or scream; she only writhed in the burning of her own making. By the time the blaze had caught the house, Margaret had lost consciousness. By the time the firefighters, summoned by a neighbor who had finally risen, reached the backyard, they found Margaret lying with the ashes of her writing, her hair so singed she appeared bald, her body so charred she was no longer recognizable.

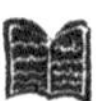

Anarchical Borderline Child

Sarah-Jean Krahn

iTS NOT ALL iN

MEEES HEAD

ANY

MORE

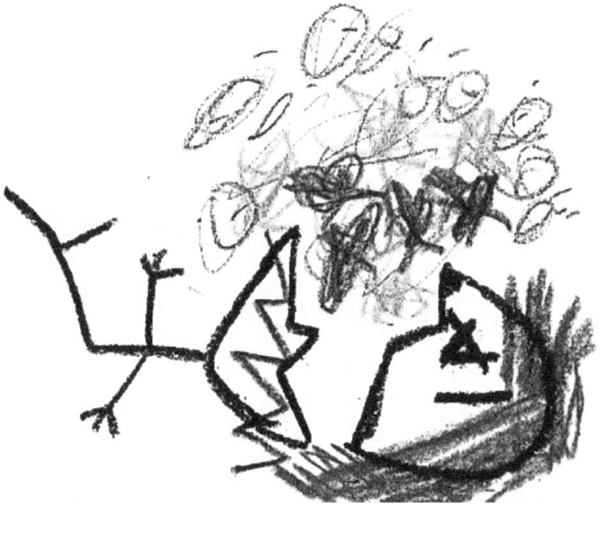

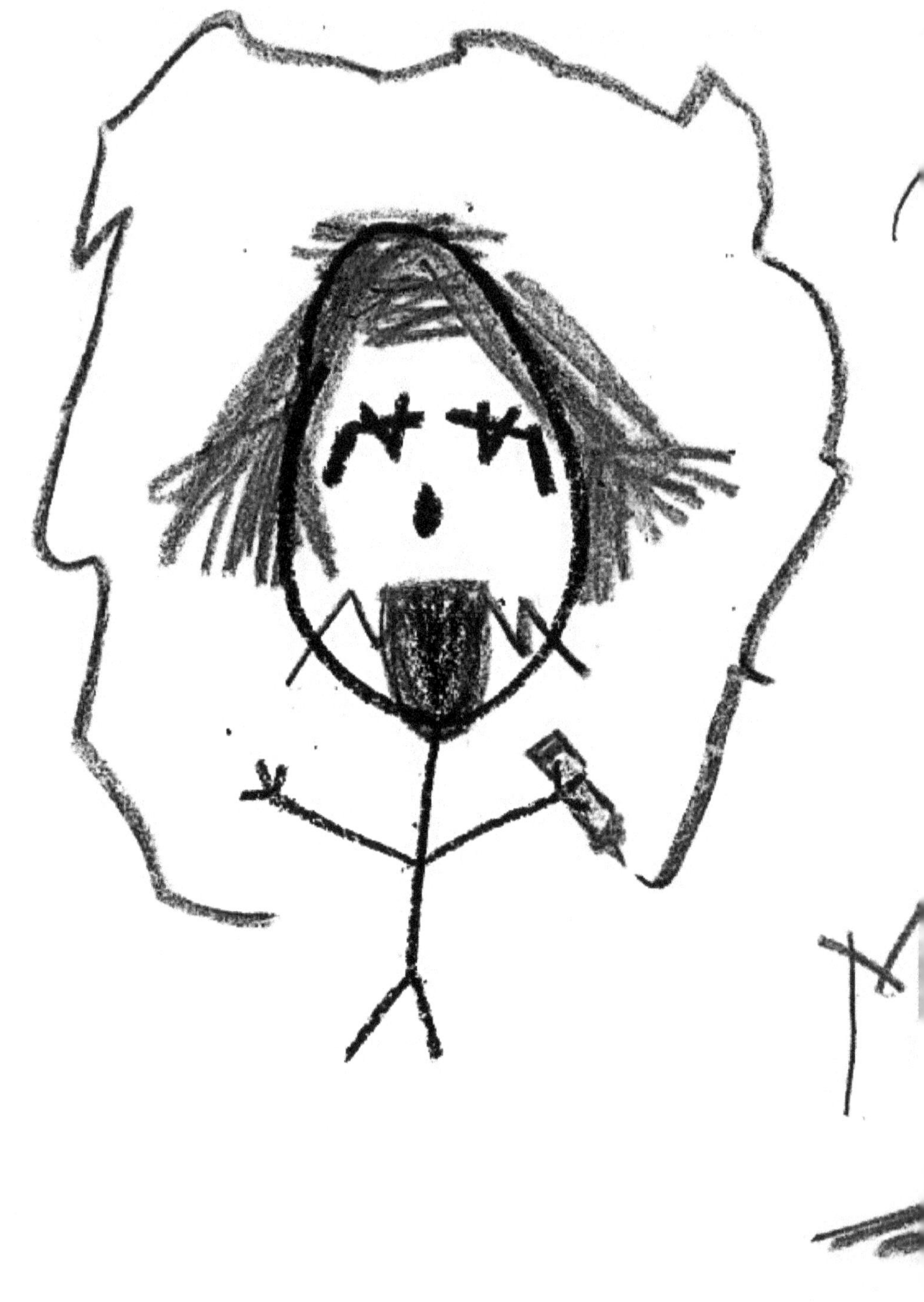

EES NOT A
LITTLE GIRL

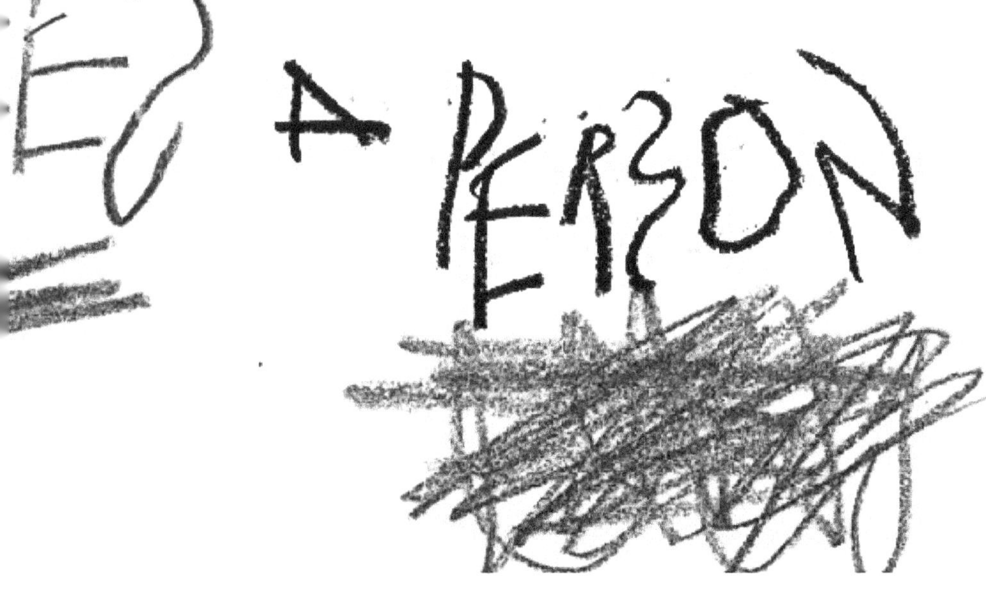

Four Poems

Mike Algera

How I Returned Here

It started with a sunrise—
I had slept in my car, parked
in a Super 8 motel, the morning
sky a pale mauve; my hangover
encumbered by birdsong and stuttering
engine, stirred by bikers
and the breakfast
crowd, by the stench of bacon
and exhaust fumes
I trailed the bacon towards a diner
went in, ordered coffee and pancakes
Giving up was never an easy occurrence
for me, and mornings were never
a good time for solitude—you get food
even when you are not hungry, and get
a waitress named Francesca
with the mortician's face and
notepad, and you yearn for the warmth
of a Maureen or a Teresa, shimmying skirt
carafe in hand—you retreat to
a booth knowing you can distance yourself,
the newspapers and menus plentiful
and a wealth of sugar packets to steal

The outside world targets you from behind glass
holding you under the cold tap of facts
I'm offered this beautiful maple tree—sentient
of plush green health and prosperity
centuries old
Bird projectiles hurl themselves like kamikazes
Hitchcock stops and stares outside my window
I marvel at my platter of buttermilk
disks, smothered in the sap of Ontario amber
I suppose I have another poem in me, turn
another morsel
into a banquet—and that's when
you order a plate of bacon; that's when
the birds really start singing; that's when
the cars stretch for miles like children at recess—
that's when you get hungry

Sandals and Socks

It's like he doesn't even care
his body has betrayed him

like some animal offering itself
to jungle hazards, begging

for death in scraps. Even the tides
dare not cross his knee high

woolly appendages, sucking
up surf and foam. He can't

remember, the last time
that he felt his toes tingle.

His big toe protrudes
from a clean tear in the sock,

swollen, parched longing
for the cool cumbersome sea.

His wife left him. I don't mean
that she left him for another man,

she ran away to her latest sewing circle
to gossip over the fabrics of one's affairs.

He hasn't been held in years
except for a fitting at Sears.

He hasn't been kissed in years.
The sea is looking awful friendly

rolling over like a huge lap dog.
Just one kiss, he says, wandering in.

One kiss. It's all I need
to sleep off this sinking feeling.

Talent

Don't let it
slip away. Don't
drag it out like
a disobedient dog,
don't toss it aside like
a pebble
in your shoe, don't
spend your life
playing catch
up with the muse.

Don't let it seal
itself up within
walls or half-
buried underneath
a cabin in the woods.
Don't shackle it
up in the attic, force
feed it fish heads
and cattle-prods, nor
the sweets of gluttony.
They are small gifts—
like a bird. They reach out
like little branches.

Before you know
it, it will turn
up missing, like a body
in a Stephen
King novel. A wasted
half measure for circling
vultures, congregating
carrion to claim.

Pizza Deliverance

Ciao! I'm Don Dominic
Corleone Macaroni and I'm your
pizza deliverance man, route 66.
Mister Hot-and-Ready. Mister
Fresh-and-Go. I preach
the gospel of sage, basil, dill
and marjoram. If honey cured
ham, then you can say that I
cured hunger. Want more
dough for your dough? Gourmet
if I may? Every pizza
is a sunrise—the earth's crust
expands and contracts to shape
the valley. Buttons of pepperoni
popping at the satin seams
of cheese cloth. Higgs boson
the topping of toppings. We kick
the competition to the curb
with the boot of Sicily. Leave
no pizza stone unturned, no topping
untouched. The science of sauces is
an art of divination, there's to-mate-o,
to-mat-toe, and then there's us—
the sauciest of saucier. Pizza deliverance 29:9

minutes or less or your money back.
We'll give you two medium sized
pizzas for five, just like Mamma Dominic
Corleone Macaroni used to make. The cacciatore
wings are catchy, the crazy bread
an obsession. There's no heaven on earth
like hell's kitchen. Come in for Monday
Munchies. Cut the cheese? Just say please.

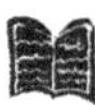

Madame Strange

Lucy Black

Come in. I'm Seraphina Finch. I'm the one and only fortune teller of Watussa Grove. You're a stranger. Nobody in this town has the audacity to step inside my parlor in broad daylight. That and your silver Caddy tell me all I need to know. What are you looking for? Amusement? Secrets? Lottery numbers? I'm sick of all that. Have a seat.

Winter's come too soon this year. It's never been this cold. The frost charms the birds and they peck at the pavement as if they could crack it open. I look for meaning in the meaningless, frost on the glass, the chatter of birds, the tarot, tea leaves, or the ashes of these cigarettes. People come to me for answers and I tell them pretty stories. Your husband is cheating on you, I say. Yes, you're going to have a little boy, I say. Sometimes they ask for love potions or healing. I grow herbs and sell them as charms. Put this in her coffee. Place this sachet under your pillow. You'd be surprised what people will ask for but it's always been this way. Granny did the same. She was a hedge witch, lived on Sand Mountain and cut the clouds with knives. She drove them into the ground and dared the storms to cross her.

That picture? Isn't she beautiful? Her name was Josephine. Our parents were literary illiterates. We called her little Joe. She had hair as thick and unruly as a pony's. No matter how many times I brushed it, ten minutes later it'd be a mess again. That's why she kept it chopped so short. Look at those scabbed knees. What a tom boy! She died a long time ago. Excuse me. No, I don't want to talk about it.

The South has a way of twisting women. It makes us tough as thorns and just as prickly. Did you notice how clean the streets are? There's an old lady who roams the sidewalks and the pavements picking up cigarette butts. Back home she taps out all the left over tobacco. Then she rolls her own. You have to admire that. It takes a special kind of guts. I imagine a fancy lady like you would curl your bleached lip right up at her. She wraps her hair in a turban and she's ten times the queen you are.

Oh, don't go. My insults are harmless. Let me see your hands. They're soft. Mine are like cracked embers. I've spent too many years out in the cold listening to the crows. See this line here? It measures out our years. Mine is so long it almost wraps around to the back. Look at yours. It's broken. You knew, didn't you? It's why you came. Too bad. I hate it for you but there's no hurry. Stick around and I'll see what I can do.

Joe had that same broken line but hers was even shorter. It never frightened her. Her favorite games were tag football and running to the river to fish. She climbed every tree from here to Alabama. But not me. I used to stare as she climbed those secret heights, afraid if I blinked even once it would cause her to fall. She laughed at me and claimed she was going to climb right up to heaven one day. Then you'll have to follow me, she'd say. You'll have no choice.

Excuse my manners, Caddy. I know I smoke like a dragon. It won't hurt you. They tell me I should quit, that it'll kill me someday. The fools. Don't they know we all have to die? Care for some coffee? We always drank it black. Sugar and cream were not allowed in the house of repression. Aunt Felicia found my tarot cards when I was fifteen. I wouldn't throw them away so she kicked me out of the house. She told everyone I was a devil worshipper. Isn't that something? Well every devil is a rebel is my friend. Have a cigarette.

Good, I'm corrupting you already. Never do what they tell you. Drive that Caddy wherever it takes you. The answers you're looking for will find you. We're all accidents of fate. Too many people look for love in the wrapping. They miss the magic right next door. In the dark all of us are warm. That's how I make money. I provide a valuable service to the love starved and the damned. Then when they're distracted I milk them for information or favors. The whole town's tied up neat in my pocket and they know it. Even the preacher has some secrets his congregation would hang him for. See these blue stockings with the black garters? They're my trademark and I know exactly what they mean. The South is still two hundred years behind the rest of the world. This is the freedom salon. That's why I keep a candle burning in the window.

Joe and I grew up in a Puritan prison. Our only escape was the library and we spent most of our time there. It was our refuge. Hypocrites take one look at a book and run screaming. I know. I'm as bitter as the dregs in this cup. It's what they did to her, you see. I can't get it out of my mind. I should have been there to save her. I didn't have any money and no one would hire me. I roamed the cold in my one ragged dress looking for daddies to give me some sugar. Meanwhile Joe was trapped in that house without me to watch over her. She was twelve years old. That year her breasts came on fast. At the beginning of the summer she was flat as a board and by the end she was miserable with all that weight. Her face began to look haggard. They had to go to Atlanta to find brassieres that would fit. The boys taunted her. You know how it is. She stopped running and climbing trees and playing football. The boys got too grabby. People began to gossip, say only one thing could make breasts grow like that. You see the kind of idiocy we had to live with? Uncle Paul told her to stay away from men. He poured so much rape into her ears she couldn't stay in the same room with a man, always hid in the back bedroom till they left. People called her names. Then at fourteen Aunt Felicia found her in the bushes kissing another girl. But they were doing more than kissing. God bless her.

It's hot as the blazes in here. Wood heat is the hottest thing there is. Let me prop open the back door, let the cold in. That's better. Nicotine makes all the details pop. See those trees? They always remind me of skeletons waving frozen arms. It's like they're screaming. The sky's too soupy yet. It'll sleet tonight. I can smell it. There's a bed and breakfast on the edge of town. Mary Talbot runs it and she'll give you the best room if you say I sent you. She knocked her old man down a well. Don't worry, he deserved it. I helped her cover it up. Old wells are the oubliettes of the South. Mary cooks the best pot roast but she's a miser when it comes to heat. Best be wrapped up tight by nine o'clock.

Where was I? Oh yeah. I met Shorty Reynolds and moved into his trailer. I heard about what was going on with Joe. The family sent her to a brainwasher to try and cure her. As if she had a disease! I stole Shorty's Ford out of the parking lot at the Mill. Rode out to the house and tried to rescue her from that hellhole but she wouldn't come to stay with me on account of him. Felicia caught me in their house packing a bag. I'll never forget it. "How dare you?" she said. "Get out of my house!" I guess it didn't help that I stole all the money out of her cookie jar. You should have heard her scream. "Look what you did bringing the devil down on us! Queers burn in hell! Don't you go with her, Josephine Finch! Do you want to burn forever and ever like your devil worshipping whore of a sister?"

You're laughing? It sounds like something out of *Deliverance*, doesn't it? What's a sophisticated cat like you doing out here in the sticks? If I'd had any sense I would have run away to New York a long time ago. How did I know? Well, let's say it's something in your smile. But who am I kidding? I couldn't leave after what they did.

Shorty got pissed at me for getting drunk and wrecking his truck. He tried to take a down payment out on me. I cut him right across his left cheek. A good scar's as pretty as a tattoo. We didn't get along after that. I moved in with his friend Fred Sunjer and we got along fine. He was one of the good ones. He was sweet as a teddy bear and loved to provide. Well a good man is hard to find so I kept him so full of sugar it killed him in the end. He lost his mind when the gossip got to him. He's still a resident at Pine Wood. I visit every Sunday.

Want some more coffee? I'm dry as a bone. Seems all the sap has run right out of me. I didn't think it'd be this hard to talk. All these stories banging around in me for years and I never told anyone what really happened. Then I tell the first stranger that comes along. But we're not really strangers are we? I think we're sisters across the Mason Dixon line. War is always a man's mess and then we have to clean it up. We're always cleaning things up. Civilization was founded on the backs of women slaving to provide shelter so men could have the leisure and luxury of exploring their souls. We've only had one for a hundred years or so and we're still getting the hang of it. Funny thing about a soul is how hard it dies. The more you try to kill it the more it cries.

They called me at work at ten thirty on Saturday, August 15. I was cutting hair at Sherry's Salon. That morning there was a pair of doves cooing on my window sill. I spent all day waiting for that damn phone to ring. Do you know what that's like? Hold my hand. Soft and hard, that's us. We're sisters of the soul.

Sherry answered the phone. Her back got all stiff. I couldn't let go of the scissors. "Sera," she said. "You better get over here." I still had the scissors in my hand when I got in the car to drive to the hospital. The family was huddled up in the emergency room but for once they didn't say a word. The nurse took me back to see her. She was so slim under all those blankets and wires. I knew it was bad from the look on the doctor's face.

"Joe," I said. "What have you done?"

She was groggy from the morphine but her eyes were bright. They were so bright.

"It's okay," she said. "I'm free now."

I threw back the covers then and I saw…

"Do you remember," she said, "When we pretended you were Wendy and I was Peter Pan?"

I can't help it. I know you understand. My God, what she did to herself! They couldn't fix it but they tried. She died on the operating table. Damn this town with its religion that kills little girls. Damn them all for throwing her away! They raised her on hatred and then murdered her for having the courage to reach out for love…

I'm sorry. It's just that I still see her smiling in my dreams, see how she must have done it… Other women came to see me after. They told me how they felt the same way sometimes. I started to understand what a curse a body can be when it's all you are to people. They think you belong to them.

I don't remember much after that. There was a spate of arson in the county. Every church in town burned to the ground. It was one long hot, endless August. They tried to blame it on me but I had a rock solid alibi and a friend who was a firebug. Simon Russell. He burned his hands making love to me. I kissed and worshiped every scar on his body. We harassed Aunt Felicia and Uncle Paul until they moved out of town. The brainwasher disappeared and they never found him. How we made the bastards pay!

But it wasn't enough. I never could find any peace. There were always more little girls and boys with that trapped fever in their eyes. There were grown men doomed to live out their lives as bachelors in empty rooms, women who were never allowed to smile in public or say hello to a child. Too many people forced to turn their backs on love. Suicides. Maybe they thought heaven would be more forgiving. I began to study how people were trapped in old ideas, how they changed faces depending on the weather or who was watching. I traded my house for this little building and I decorated it to suit a particular taste. Sin is such a potent attractor. I had Simon paint that sign out front that says Madame Strange. That's what they always called me so I used it. My reputation grew and grew. People began to come at all hours of the night to confess or ask for help. I began to work… and my Magnum Opus is almost complete.

Do you see now? I own this town. The Devil taught me how. Every secret, every shame, every last drop of their desire is right here in the palm of my hand. Gender, color or creed is no more important to me than the roll of these dice. I love them and hate them all. I give them the freedom to do what they will. I tell them what they need to hear if it helps them reach for one ounce of freedom. And behind all that sweetness lurks the poison that's been building to a head. It's about to explode. Didn't you see the doves in the yard? They mate for life.

Let me tell you a secret about yourself. There's someone you left behind. You drove all this way in that silver Cadillac to knock on my door. It doesn't matter why. Turn that car around and go back where you came from. Make the bastards love you. It's the only way you'll ever be free. Go on. Don't let the ice catch you here. There's something going down tonight you don't want to be a part of. Remember me and Joe if you can. Show me your hand again. Look at that, we traded. I took your broken line.

Tell whoever's waiting that Seraphina sent you.

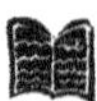

A Selection of Works on Paper and Canvas

Michael Tice

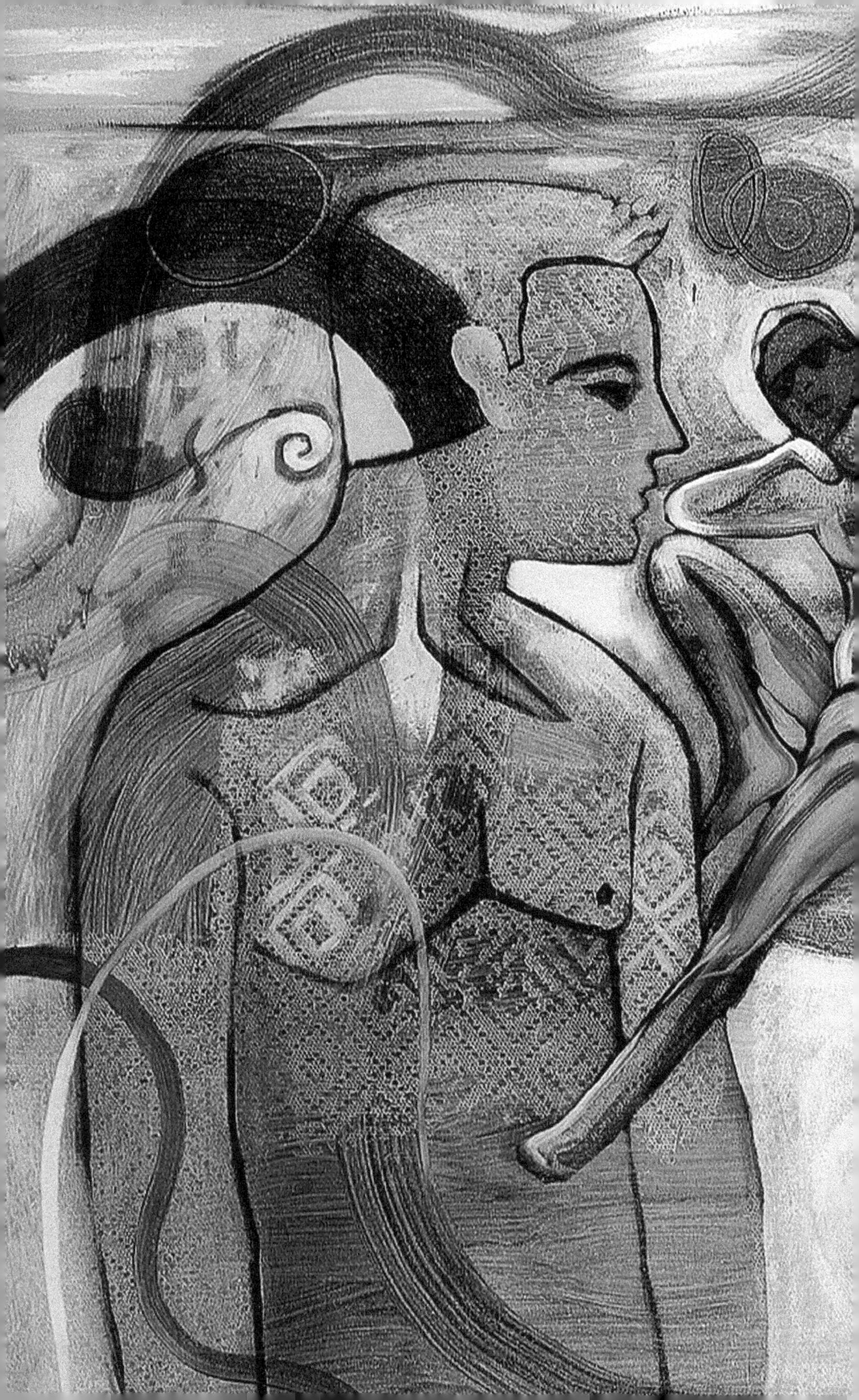

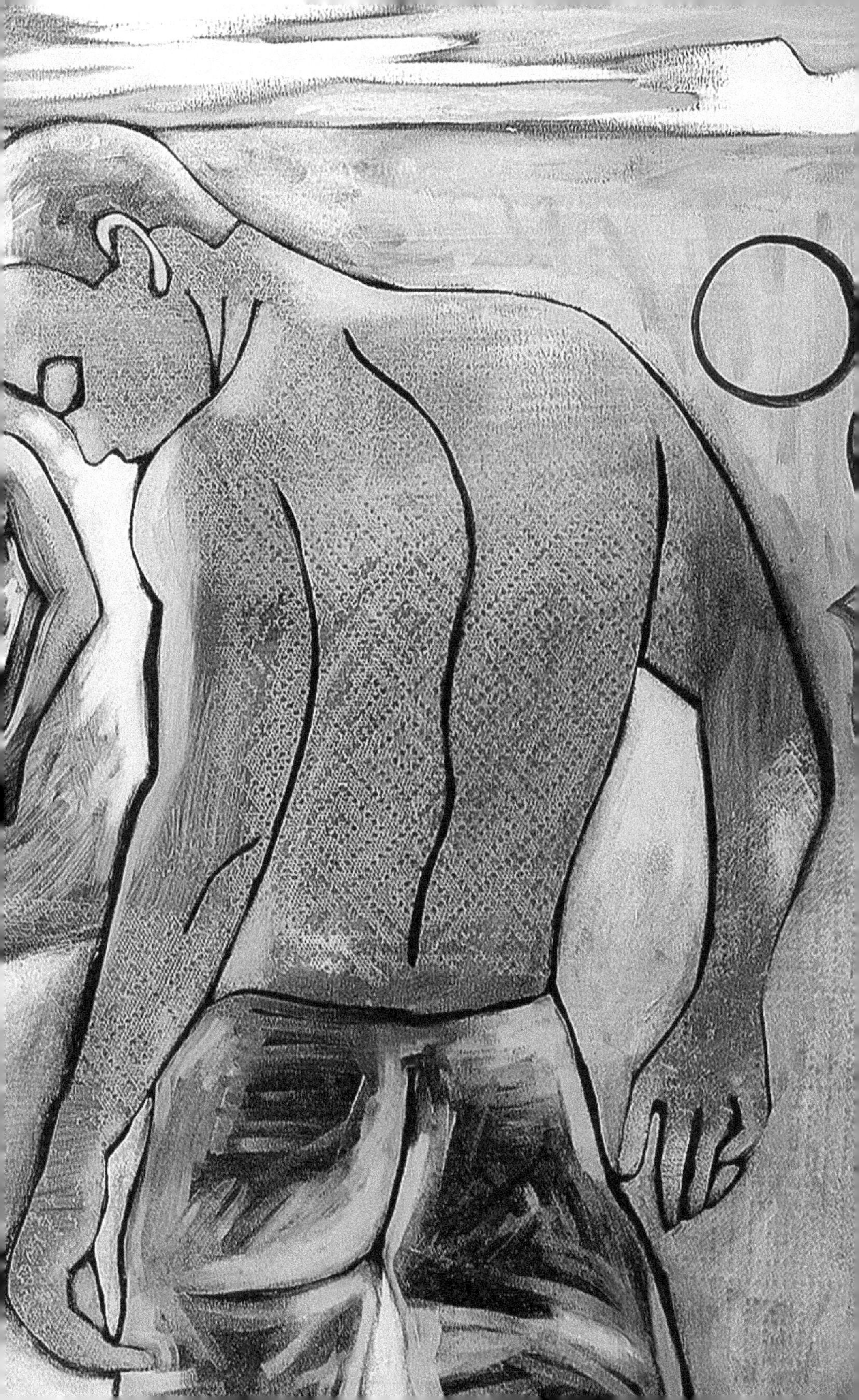

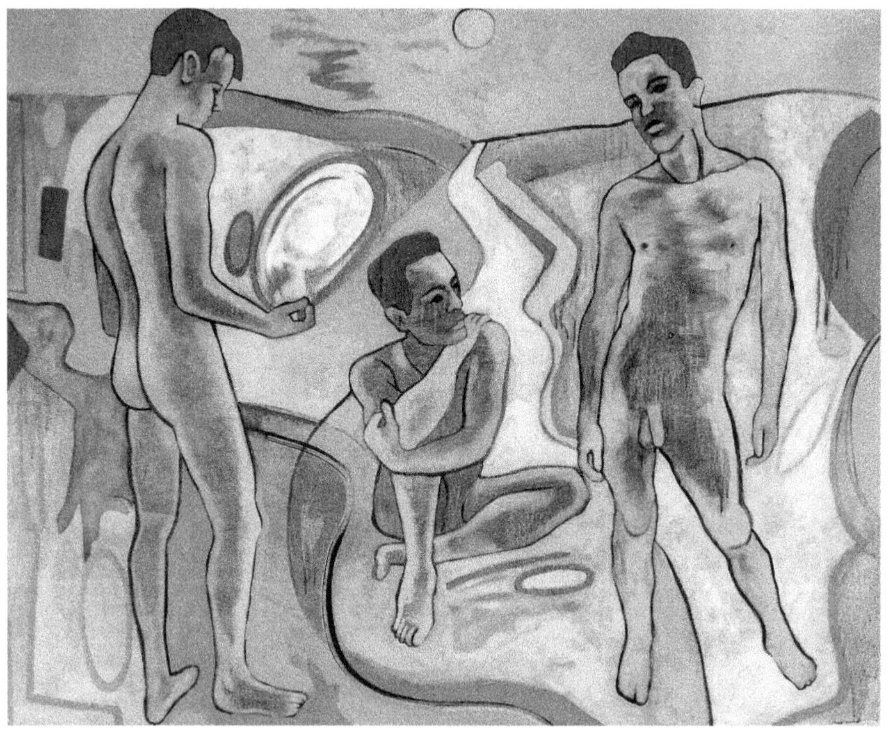

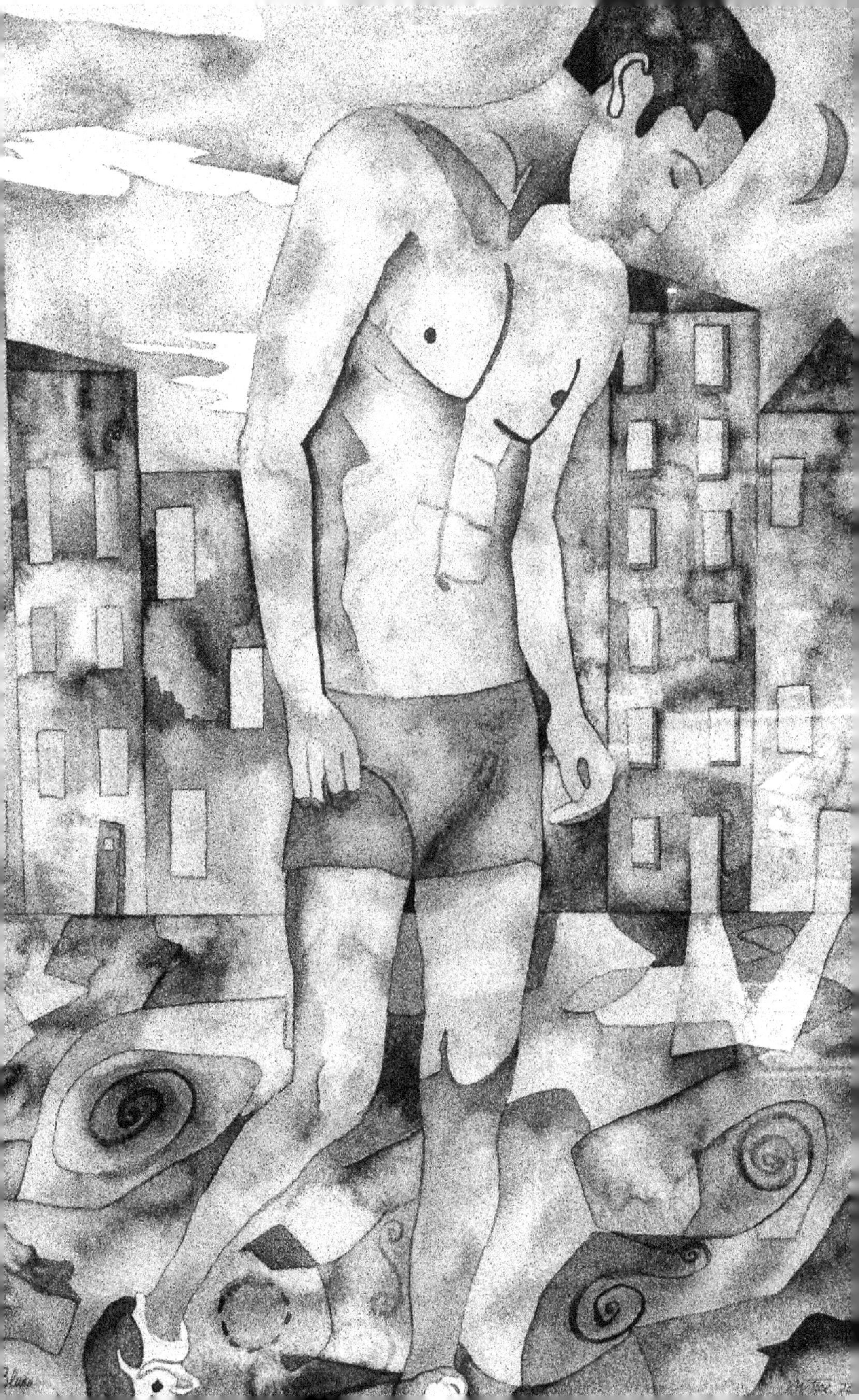

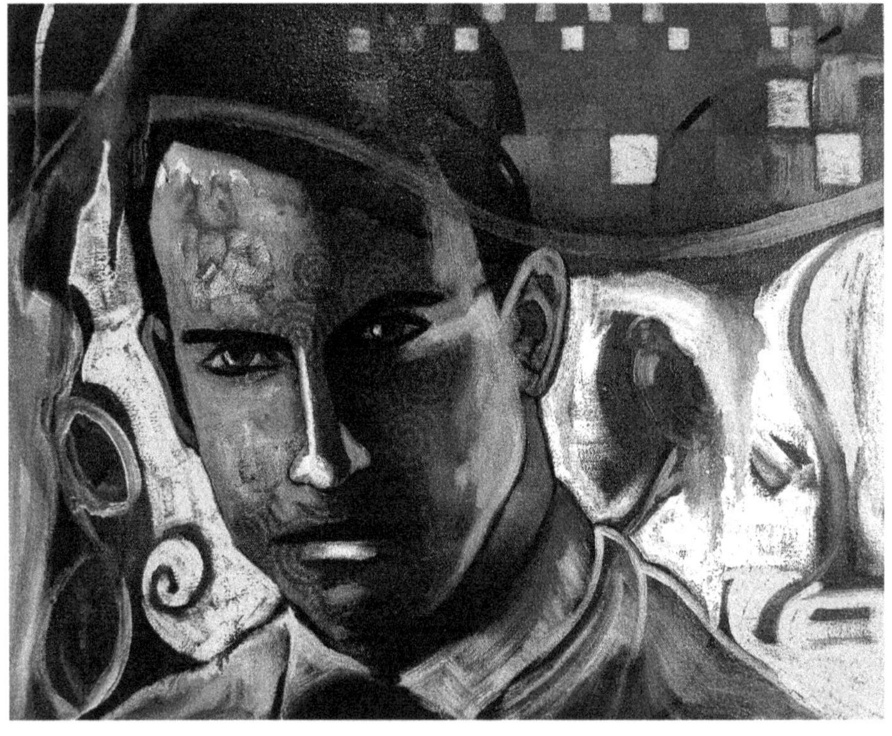

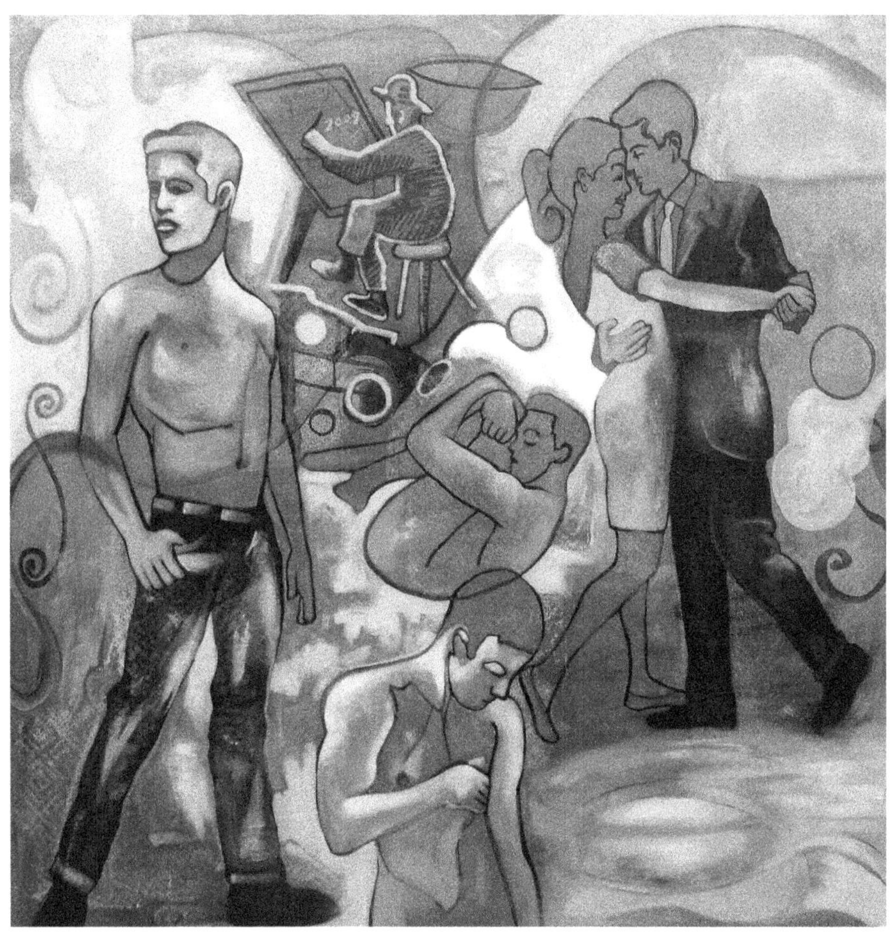

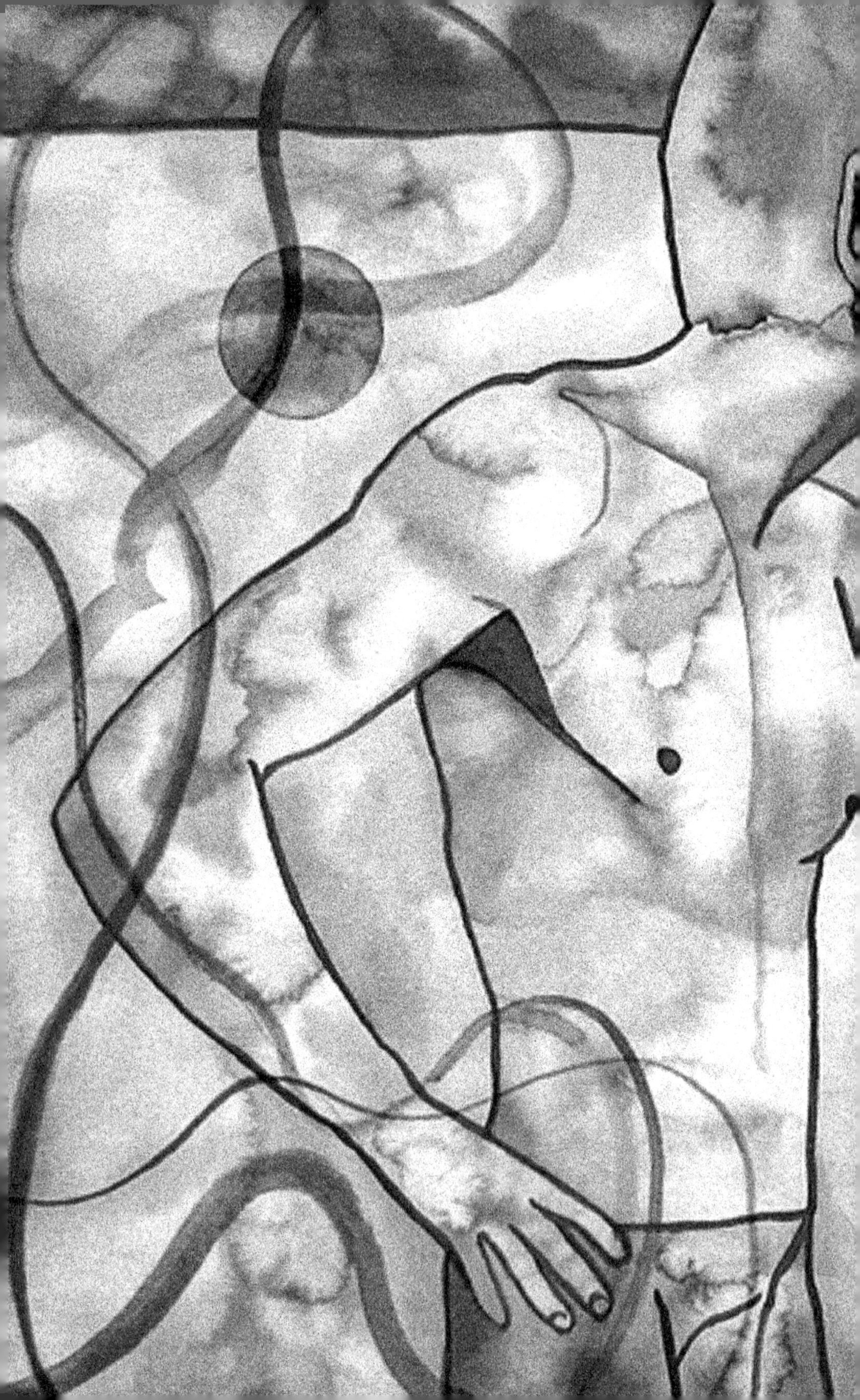

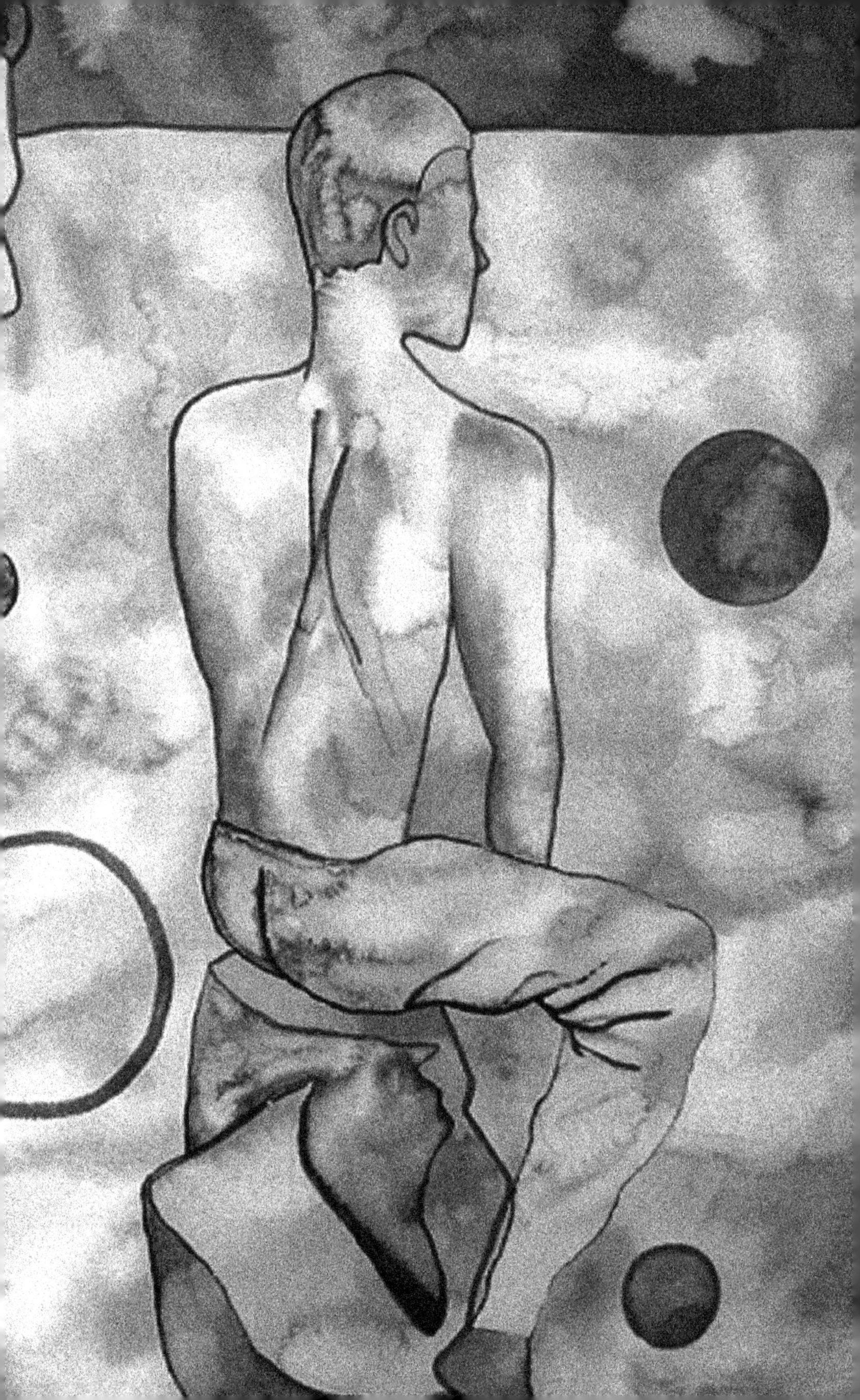

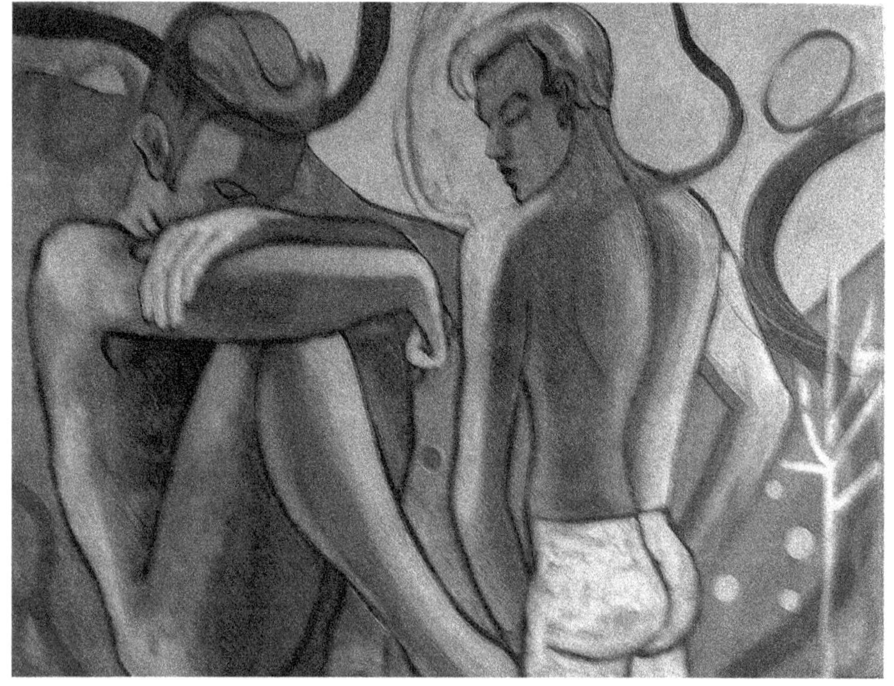

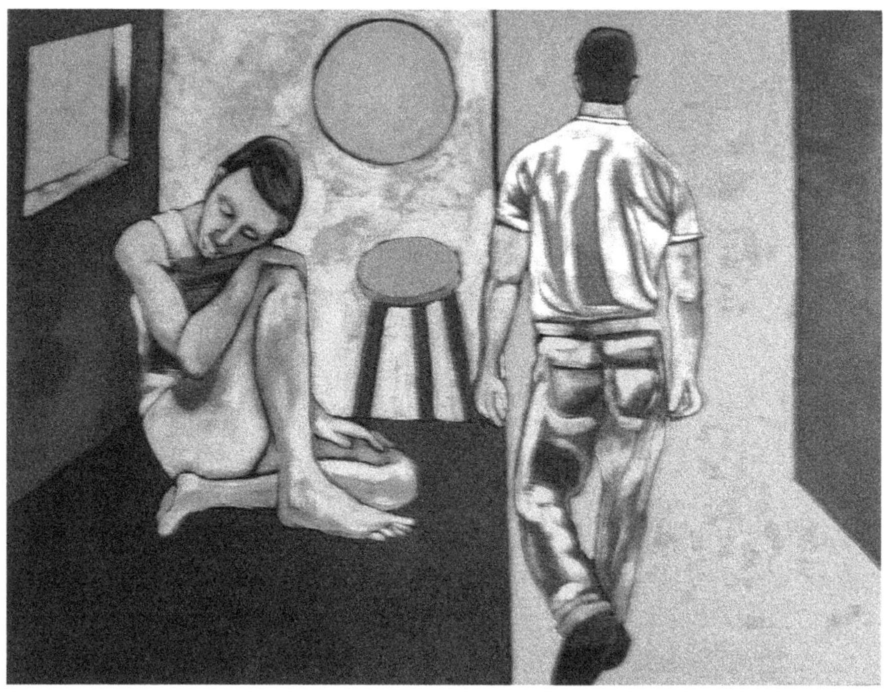

Contributors

Mike Algera has authored three poetry collections: *Old Gods for New*, *Outskirts*, and *Like Indigenous Tiger*. He has been published by *Arc Poetry Magazine*, BareBack Lit, Hamilton Arts & Letters, Nostrovia Poetry, Word Salad, and Cyclamens & Swords Publishing. He lives in Hamilton with his high maintenance dog, Grendel. His favourite themes include dysfunctional families, Oriental mysticism, vigilante justice, love and love in all of the wrong places. His home away from home is in digital la-la land, at www.mikealgera.com.

Jack Bates is an award winning writer. He has written for stage, screen, and local television. He's also quite popular in the crime fiction arena.

Lucy Black writes short stories that exist somewhere within the worlds of southern gothic and speculative fiction. Her work has appeared or is forthcoming from *Red Truck Review*, Severest Inks, and New Lit Salon Press. She lives and works in Chattooga County, Georgia.

Brian Centrone is the author of the novel *An Ordinary Boy* and the short story collections *I Voted for Biddy Schumacher: Mismatched Tales from the Mind of Brian Centrone* and *Erotica*. Four of his One-Act plays have been produced for the stage as part of the National Endowment for the Arts'

The Big Read program. His writing has appeared in numerous anthologies, literary and arts journals, newspapers, and online. He is the Co-Founder and Publisher of New Lit Salon Press and has taught writing and literature at The Massillon Museum, SUNY/Westchester Community College, and New York University. Visit Brian at www.briancentrone.com and follow him @briancentrone.

M.P. Diederich was born somewhere in New England in 1985. Despite his interest in dangerous subjects, he is not currently under FBI surveillance. He studied English and Creative Writing at Fordham University in New York City while seriously considering joining the French Foreign Legion. He currently lives in Brooklyn, where he's trying to introduce more green vegetables into his diet and maybe go for a run every once in a while.

Reymond Drew is an emerging writer originally from the East Coast, now living on the West. He uses his art as a subversive weapon to generate conversation about the social and economic politics of living as a transgender man. When he's not writing or running his tiny care package business, he tries to find time to enjoy art, food, nature and dear friends.

Casey Ellis graduated from Manhattanville College in 2004, where he wrote a senior thesis on ethical issues in Oscar Wilde's *The Picture of Dorian Gray*. He received a Masters in English from the University at Buffalo in 2006, with a thesis on the language of the fool characters in Shakespeare's major tragedies. He is currently an adjunct with the English departments of Westchester Community College and Berkeley College, and a verbal skills tutor with Huntington Learning Center. Whenever possible, Casey updates his literary blog *"Tolle, lege!"* (http://caseyellis66.wordpress.com/). In addition to this collection, Casey was the line editor of two previous New Lit Salon Press collections: *Southern Gothic: New Tales of the South* and *Behind the Yellow Wallpaper: New Tales of Madness*. He is the editor of the upcoming NLSP collection *Startling Sci-Fi: New Tales of the Beyond*.

Casey would like to gratefully acknowledge his friend Samuel Ferri, for his editorial contributions to "The Creature from the Lake."

Stefanie Freele is the author of two short story collections, *Feeding Strays*, with Lost Horse Press and *Surrounded by Water*, with Press 53. Stefanie's published and forthcoming work can be found in *Witness*, *Glimmer Train*, *Mid-American Review*, *Wigleaf*, *Western Humanities Review*, *Sou'wester*, *Chattahoochee Review*, *The Florida Review*, *Quarterly West*, and *American Literary Review*. www.stefaniefreele.com.

Jessica Hoard is a writer, photographer, actor, cat farmer, and guru—and pretty much anything else that can't be parlayed into a real job—from Memphis, TN. Her work has appeared in numerous publications, including *55 words*, *Breath and Shadow*, *Pear Noir!*, *Miss Guided Magazine*, *Tiny Lights*, *Greatest Uncommon Denominator*, and *Short, Fast, and Deadly*. Follow @jesshoard for her devastating insights and semi-lucid rantings.

Sarah-Jean Krahn is the co-founder and Managing Editor of the feminist creative writing journal *S/tick*. Her award-winning writing has appeared in *dead (g)end(er)*, *ditch*, *Herizons*, *The Missing Slate*, *Zest*, various anthologies, and the academic journal *Feminist Studies*. She holds an MA in Cultural Studies and Critical Theory from McMaster University. More of her creations can be viewed online at www.sarahjeancreates.com. This is her debut for published artwork.

Nathan Mark Phillips is a digital artist who lives in the Tampa Bay area of Florida. His hometown is Cleveland, TN. His background has significant impact on his thoughts as expressed in his Art: Nathan is from the South; He is a student of theology, psychology and sociology, and enjoys Pop Culture. He has spent his professional life working in human services with the severely mentally ill, those impacted by substance abuse or family crisis. He lives a very happy life with his husband, the best of friends and a wonderful family. In 2013 his work was published in *Southern Gothic: New Tales of the South* from New Lit Salon Press.

Dan Ress lives in Colorado with his wife and his dog. When he's not reading, writing, or teaching, he is often playing music, wandering in the mountains, traveling, or seeking to overcome the awkwardness of writing about himself in the third person. He is fascinated by non-violent revolutions, although he grants that they have fewer explosions. You can find some of Dan's work published at Jersey Devil Press, Imaginaire, and Apocrypha and Abstractions. Also, feel free to visit his website at http://thesolidshade.wordpress.com for more writing or just for greater insight into his odd philosophy and even odder sensibility.

John Rodzvilla is an artist, writer, publisher and teacher. He currently teaches at Emerson College. His work has appeared in *Harvard Review*, *McSweeney's Internet Tendency*, *Verbatim* and *Bad Robot Poetry*.

Michele Seminara is a poet and yoga teacher from Sydney. Her writing has appeared in publications such as *Bluepepper*, *Tincture Journal*, *Regime*, and *Verity La*. She is also a poetry reader for *Verity La*, as well as being the journal's incoming managing editor. She blogs at http://micheleseminara.wordpress.com/ and is on twitter @SeminaraMichele.

P.J. Schaefer earned her Ph.D. in American literature at Fordham University, New York and teaches at SUNY Westchester Community College. She is a published freelance writer and editor of long and short mainstream fiction and nonfiction, and her works have appeared in such publications as *Troika*, *Dogsongs*, *Elements*, *Ink.*, *Poor Katie's Almanac*, *Offshore: Northeast Boating*, *Boston Parents' Paper*, *Big Apple Parent*, *Children's Writer*, *Family Times*, *Naturally Women Magazine*, and *Camping Today*. Her academic publications include essays for *The Western Journal of Black Studies*, *The Journal of Black Studies*, *A.T.Q.: 19th Century American Literature and*

Culture, The Facts on File Companion to the American Short Story, Literary Themes for Students: War and Peace, The Facts on File Companion to the American Novel, and *Teaching English in the Two-Year College.*

Luke Spooner a.k.a. 'Carrion House' and 'Hoodwink House,' currently lives and works in the South of England. Having graduated from the University of Portsmouth with a first class degree he is now a full time illustrator and writer for just about any project that peaks his interest. Despite regular forays into children's books and fairy tales, for which he has won awards for literary and artistic merit, his true love is anything macabre, melancholy or dark in nature and essence. He believes that the job of putting someone else's words into a visual form, to accompany and support their text, is a massive responsibility as well as being something he truly treasures.

Michael Tice has shown his work frequently since the early 1970's. He has had many solo exhibitions and has been included in numerous group shows. He has a BFA from the University of South Carolina and has done graduate work at the University of North Carolina and New York University. *Retrospective*, the first monograph on the artist, was published by New Lit Salon Press with bd-studios.com. He lives and works in New York. Visit Michael at http://www.michaeltice.com.

John Vicary began publishing poetry in the fifth grade and has been writing ever since. A contributor to many compendiums, his most recent credentials include short fiction in the collections *Midnight Circus, We Were Heroes* and *Temporary Skeletons*. He has stories in upcoming issues of *Boktor Magazine* and *Halfway Down the Stairs*. John enjoys playing piano and lives in rural Michigan with his family. You can read more of his work at keppiehed.com.

About NLSP

We are New Lit Salon Press and we create books. We are writers. We are artists. We are makers with a mission: to publish the best and brightest, to amplify the voice of a generation lost in the void of a system concerned only about million dollar bestsellers. We look to the past but move boldly towards the future.

Founded by Brian Centrone (Publisher) and Jordan M. Scoggins (Creative Director) in 2012, New Lit Salon Press is based on the principle that Words and Art can and should coexist. NLSP is committed to publishing essays, stories, poems, novels, and art from undiscovered writers and promising artists who struggle to thrive in a marketplace that fails to recognize their talent. We believe in what you do.

The world of publishing is changing. NLSP not only recognises that but embraces it. To meet the demands of the evolving marketplace, NLSP releases are available on all major ebook platforms. However, because we are suckers for the printed page and we love the artistry of a physical object, we also produce print-on-demand trade editions of select titles.

With over 20 collective years of experience in creative, publishing, technology, and academic fields, we bring a unique skill set to the table. Our comprehensive approach is designed to nurture new and unheard talent in ways most indie publishers do not. We love what we do (and hope you do too).

We are artists. We are writers. We are NLSP and we create books.

Also available from NLSP

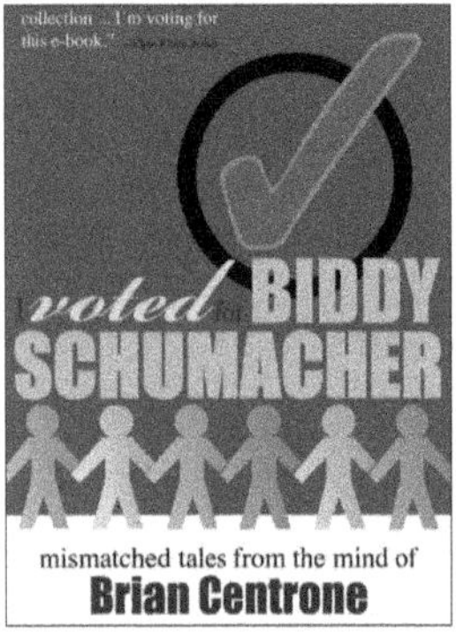

I Voted for Biddy Schumacher: Mismatched Tales from the Mind of Brian Centrone

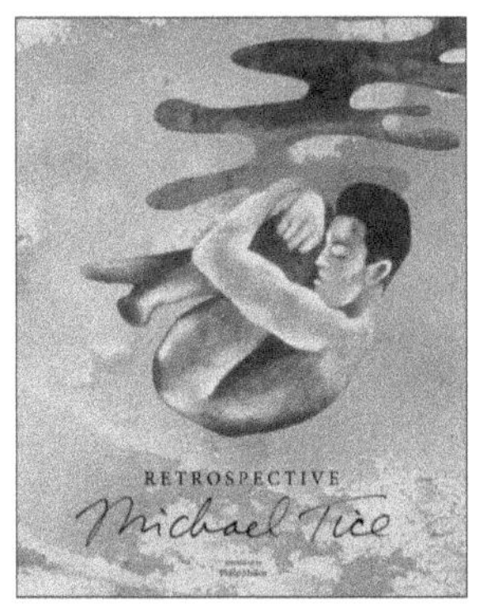

Retrospective
by Michael Tice

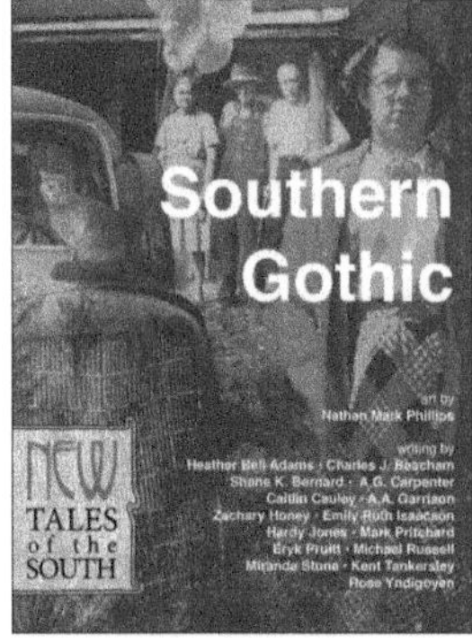

Southern Gothic: New Tales of the South
edited by Brian Centrone and Jordan M. Scoggins

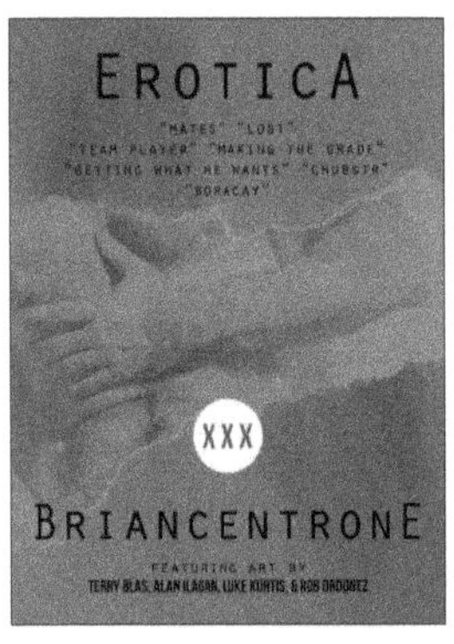

Erotica
by Brian Centrone

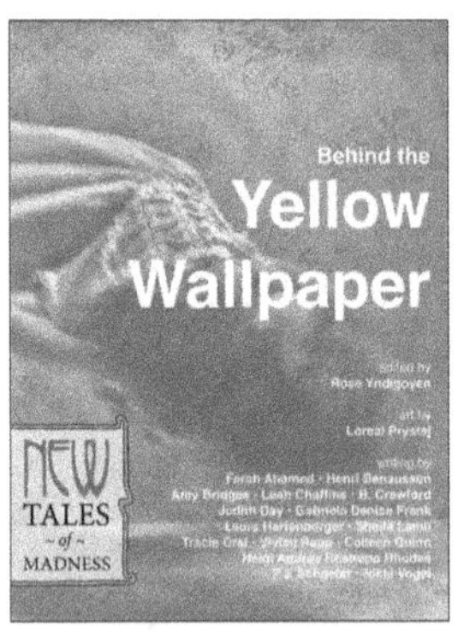

Behind the Yellow Wallpaper: New Tales of Madness
edited by Rose Yndigoyen

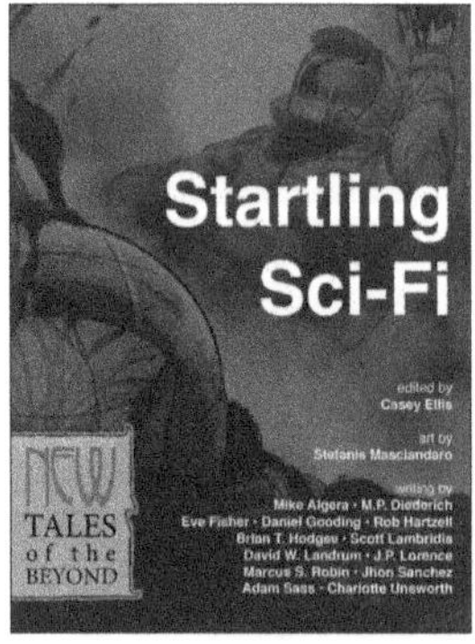

Startling Sci-Fi: New Tales of the Beyond
edited by Casey Ellis